Contents

Introduction

Welcome to NVQ/SVQ CAA Diploma Level 2 Painting and Decorating!

Painting and Decorating combines many different practical and visual skills with a knowledge of specialised materials and techniques. This book will introduce you to the construction trade and covers the knowledge you will need to begin work at height, prepare surfaces, complete specialist decorative effects and work with surface coverings such as paint and paper.

About this book

This book has been produced to help you build a sound knowledge and understanding of all aspects of the Diploma and NVQ requirements associated with painting and decorating.

The information in this book covers what you will need to attain your Level 2 qualification in Painting and Decorating. Each chapter of the book relates to a particular unit of the CAA Diploma and provides the information needed to form the required knowledge and understanding of that area. The book is also designed to support those undertaking the NVQ at Level 2.

This book has been written based on a concept used with Carillion Training Centres for many years. The concept is about providing learners with the necessary information they need to support their studies and at the same time ensuring the information is presented in a style that is both manageable and relevant.

This book will also be a useful reference tool for you in your professional life once you have gained your qualifications and are a practising painter and decorator.

This introduction will introduce the construction industry and the qualifications you can find in it, alongside the qualifications available.

About the construction industry

Construction means creating buildings and services. These might be houses, hospitals, schools, offices, roads, bridges, museums, prisons, train stations, airports, monuments – and anything else you can think of that needs designing and building! What about an Olympic stadium? The 2012 London games will bring a wealth of construction opportunity to the UK and so it is an exciting time to be getting involved.

In the UK, 2.2 million people work in the construction industry – more than in any other – and it is constantly expanding and developing. There are more choices and opportunities than ever before. Your career doesn't have to end in the UK either – what about taking the skills and experience you are developing abroad? Construction is a career you can take with you wherever you go. There's always going to be something that needs building!

The construction industry is made up of countless companies and businesses which all provide different services and materials. An easy way to divide these companies into categories is according to their size.

- A small company is defined as having between 1 and 49 members of staff.
- A medium company consists of between 50 and 249 members of staff.
- A large company has 250 or more people working for it.

A business might even consist of only a single member of staff (a sole trader).

Different types of construction work

There are four main types of construction work:

new work – this refers to a building that is about to be or has just been built

maintenance work – this is when an existing building is kept up to an acceptable standard by fixing anything that is damaged so that it does not fall into disrepair

refurbishment/renovation work – this generally refers to an existing building that has fallen into a state of disrepair and is then brought up to standard by repair work being carried out. It also refers to an existing building that is to be used for a different purpose, for example changing an old bank into a pub

restoration work – this refers to an existing building that has fallen into a state of disrepair and is then brought back to its original condition or use.

These four types of work can fall into one of two categories depending upon who is paying for the work:

- **public** – work that is paid for by the government, as is the case with most schools and hospitals, etc.
- **private** – work that is paid for by a private client and can range from extensions on existing houses to new houses or buildings.

Jobs and careers

Jobs and careers in the construction industry fall mainly into one of four categories:

- **building** – the physical construction (making) of a structure. It also involves the maintenance, restoration and refurbishment of structures

- **civil engineering** – the construction and maintenance of work such as roads, railways, bridges etc.
- **electrical engineering** – the installation and maintenance of electrical systems and devices such as lights, power sockets and electrical appliances etc.
- **mechanical engineering** – the installation and maintenance of things such as heating, ventilation and lifts.

The category that is the most relevant to your course is building.

What is a building?

There are of course lots of very different types of building, but the main types are:

- **residential** – houses, flats etc.
- **commercial** – shops, supermarkets etc.
- **industrial** – warehouses, factories etc.

These types of building can be further broken down by the height or number of storeys that they have (one storey being the level from floor to ceiling):

- **low-rise** – a building with one to three storeys
- **medium-rise** – a building with four to seven storeys
- **high-rise** – a building with seven storeys or more.

Buildings can also be categorised according to the number of other buildings they are attached to:

- **detached** – a building that stands alone and is not connected to any other building
- **semi-detached** – a building that is joined to one other building and shares a dividing wall, called a party wall
- **terraced** – a row of three or more buildings that are joined together, of which the inner buildings share two party walls.

Building requirements

Every building must meet the minimum requirements of the building reulations. The purpose of building regulations is to ensure that safe and healthy buildings are constructed for the public and that conservation (the preservation of the environment and the wildlife) is taken into account when they are being constructed. Building regulations enforce a minimum standard of building work and ensure that the materials used are of a good standard and fit for purpose.

What makes a good building?

When a building is designed, there are certain things that need to be taken into consideration, such as:

- security
- warmth
- safety

- light
- privacy
- ventilation.

A well-designed building will meet the minimum standards for all of the considerations above and will also be built in line with building regulations.

Qualifications for the construction industry

There are many ways of entering the construction industry, but the most common method is as an apprentice.

Apprenticeships

You can become an apprentice by being employed:

- directly by a construction company which will send you to college
- by a training provider, such as Carillion, which combines construction training with practical work experience.

ConstructionSkills is the national training organisation for construction in the UK and is responsible for setting training standards.

The framework of an apprenticeship is based around an NVQ (or SVQ in Scotland). These qualifications are developed and approved by industry experts and will measure your practical skills and job knowledge on-site.

You will also need to achieve:

- a technical certificate
- the ConstructionSkills health and safety test
- the appropriate level of functional skills assessment
- an Employers' Rights and Responsibilities briefing.

You will also need to achieve the right qualifications to get on a construction site, including qualifying for the CSCS card scheme (see page 4).

CAA Diploma

The Construction Awards Alliance (CAA) Diploma was launched on 1 August 2008 to replace Construction Awards. They aim to make you:

- more skilled and knowledgeable
- more confident with moving across projects, contracts and employers.

The CAA Diploma is a common testing strategy with knowledge tests for each unit, a practical assignment and the Global Online Assessment (GOLA) test.

The CAA Diploma meets the requirements of the new Qualifications and Credit Framework (QCF) which bases a qualification on the number of credits (with ten learning hours gaining one credit):

- Award (1 to 12 credits)
- Certificate (13 to 36 credits)
- Diploma (37+ credits)

As part of the CAA Diploma you will gain the skills needed for the NVQ as well as the functional skills knowledge you will need to complete your qualification.

National Vocational Qualifications (NVQs)

NVQs are available to anyone, with no restrictions on age, length or type of training, although learners below a certain age can only perform certain tasks. There are different levels of NVQ (for example 1, 2, 3), which in turn are broken down into units of competence. NVQs are not like traditional examinations in which someone sits an exam paper. An NVQ is a 'doing' qualification, which means it lets the industry know that you have the knowledge, skills and ability to actually 'do' something.

NVQs are made up of both mandatory and optional units and the number of units that you need to complete for an NVQ depends on the level and the occupation.

NVQs are assessed in the workplace, and several types of evidence are used:

- witness testimony provided by individuals who have first-hand knowledge of your work and performance relating to the NVQ
- your performance can be observed a number of times in the workplace
- historical evidence means that you can use evidence from past achievements or experience, if it is directly related to the NVQ
- assignments or projects can be used to assess your knowledge and understanding
- photographic evidence showing you performing various tasks in the workplace can be used, providing it is authenticated by your supervisor.

Functional Skills

Throughout this book you will find references to Functional Skills.

Functional skills are processes of representing, analysing and interpreting information. They are the skills needed to work independently in everyday life and are transferable to any given context. We will focus on the mathematics and English skills specifically in a construction context, so that you can identify and practise them by working through the units of the book. The references are headed **FM** for mathematics and **FE** for English. You will also use speaking and listening skills in your learning, which will support you through the programme. If you have any questions on how the skills fit into your learning, please speak to your tutor(s).

Carillion would like to thank Stephen Olsen and Kevin Jarvis for their hard work and dedication in preparing the content of this book. Carillion would like to thank John McLaughlin Harvie for preparing Functional Skills references.

Pearson Education Limited would like to thank Brian Bibby and Nicole Simpson of Furness College and John Spalding of Fareham College for the excellent technical feedback.

Introduction

Functional skills

This feature is designed to support you with your functional skills, by identifying opportunities in your work where you will be able to practise your functional skills.

Remember

This highlights key facts or concepts, sometimes from earlier in the text, to remind you of important things you will need to think about

Find out

These are short activities and research opportunities, designed to help you gain further information about, and understanding of, a topic area

Features of this book

This book has been fully illustrated with artworks and photographs. These will help to give you more information about a concept or a procedure, as well as helping you to follow a step-by-step procedure or identify a tool or material.

This book also contains a number of different features to help your learning and development.

Did you know?

This feature gives you interesting facts about the building trade

Key term

These are new or difficult words. They are picked out in **bold** in the text and then defined in the margin

Safety tip

This feature gives you guidance for working safely on the tasks in this book

Working life

This feature gives you a chance to read about and debate a real-life work scenario or problem. Why has the situation occurred? What would you do?

FAQ

These are frequently asked questions appearing at the end of each unit to answer your questions with informative answers from the experts

Check it out

A series of questions at the end of each unit to check your understanding. Some of these questions may support the collecting of evidence for the NVQ

Getting ready for assessment

This feature provides guidance for preparing for the practical assessment. It will give you advice on using the theory you have learned about in a practical way

Check your knowledge

This is a series of multiple choice questions in the style of the GOLA end of unit tests at the end of each unit.

Safe working practices in construction

Health and safety is a vital part of all construction work. All work should be completed in a way that is safe not only for the individual worker, but also for the other workers on the site, people near by and the final users of the building.

Every year in the construction industry over 100 people are killed or seriously injured as a result of the work that they do. There are thousands more who suffer from work-related health problems, such as dermatitis, asbestosis, industrial asthma, vibration white finger (see pages 10–11) and deafness. Therefore, learning as much as you can about health and safety is very important.

This unit supports NVQ units QCF01 Conform to general workplace safety and QCF03 Move and handle resources. This unit contains material that supports TAP Unit 1: Erect and dismantle working platforms, and also contains material that supports the delivery of the five generic units.

This unit will cover the following learning outcomes:

- Health and safety regulations roles and responsibilities
- Accident, first aid and emergency procedures and reporting
- Hazards on construction sites
- Health and hygiene
- Safe handling of materials and equipment
- Basic working platforms
- Working with electricity
- Using appropriate PPE
- Fire and emergency procedures
- Safety signs and notices.

Key terms

Legislation – a law or set of laws passed by Parliament, often called an Act

Hazardous – something or a situation that is dangerous or unsafe

Subcontractors – workers who have been hired by the main contractor to carry out works, usually specialist works

Supplier – a company that supplies goods, materials or services

Access – entrance, a way in

Egress – exit, a way out

Omission – something that has not been done or has been missed out

K1. Health and safety regulations – roles and responsibilities

Health and safety **legislation** is there not just to protect you – it also states what you must and must not do to ensure that no workers are placed in a situation **hazardous** to themselves or others. You will also use codes of practice and guidance notes (produced by the HSE and by companies themselves). You must be familiar with the duties of both employers and employees under the acts.

The Health and Safety at Work Act 1974 (HASAWA)

HASAWA applies to all types and places of work and to employers, employees, self-employed people, **subcontractors** and even **suppliers**. The Act protects people at work and the general public. HASAWA is designed to ensure health, safety and welfare for all persons at work and the general public. It also controls the use, handling, storage and transportation of explosives and highly flammable substances and the release of noxious/offensive substances into the atmosphere.

Employer's duties	Provide a safe place to work with safe plant and machinery. Provide safe **access** and **egress** to and from the work area. Information, training and supervision supplied to all employees. A written safety policy supplied and risk assessments carried out. PPE provided to all employees free of charge. Health and safety assured when handling, storing and transporting materials and substances. Involve trade union safety representatives, where appointed, in all health and safety matters.
Employee's duties	Must take reasonable care for their own health and safety, and the health and safety of anyone who may be affected by their acts or **omissions**. Co-operate with employer and other persons to meet the law, not use (or misuse) materials provided for their safety and report hazards or accidents.
Supplier's duties	Make sure articles are designed, constructed and fully tested so that they are safe to use, handle, transport and store. Information should be provided on all of these to the user.

Table 1.1 Duties and responsibilities

Find out

Use the Internet to find out more about contacting the HSE and the incidents that must be reported to them.

Health and Safety Executive (HSE)

The HSE is the government body responsible for the encouragement, regulation and enforcement of health, safety and welfare in the workplace in the UK and it enforces HASAWA and other laws through inspectors who can prosecute people or companies that break the law.

The HSE is responsible for encouraging, regulating and enforcing health and safety in the workplace in the UK. As part of this it should provide information and advice for employers and employees. The enforcement of HASAWA is usually delegated to local government bodies, such as county or district councils.

HSE inspectors have the authority to enter and examine any premises at any time, taking samples and possession of any dangerous article/substance. They can issue improvement notices, ordering a company to solve a problem in a certain time, or issue a prohibition notice stopping all work until the site is safe.

Construction (Design and Management) Regulations 2007

The Construction (Design and Management) Regulations 2007 are designed to help improve safety.

Employers must plan, manage and monitor work, ensuring employees are competent and provided with training and information. They must also provide adequate welfare facilities for workers. There are also specific requirements relating to lighting, excavations and traffic.

Employees must check their own competence and co-operate to co-ordinate work safely, reporting any obvious risks.

Clients must check that their appointees are competent, suitable management arrangements are made for welfare facilities and that sufficient time and resources are allowed for all stages.

Provision and Use of Work Equipment Regulations 1998 (PUWER)

These regulations cover all new or existing **work equipment**. PUWER covers starting, stopping, regular use, transport, repair, modification, servicing and cleaning of equipment.

The general duties of the Act require equipment to be used and maintained in suitable and safe conditions by a trained person. It should be fitted with appropriate warnings and be able to be isolated from sources of energy.

In addition, the Act also requires access to dangerous parts of machinery to be prevented or controlled. Suitable controls must be provided for stopping and starting of work equipment, in particular emergency stopping and braking systems should be installed. Sufficient lighting must be in place for operating equipment.

Did you know?

The HSE must be contacted if an accident occurs that results in death or major injury. The report must be followed up by a written report in ten days (form F2508).

Did you know?

On large projects, a person is appointed as the CDM co-ordinator. This person has overall responsibility for compliance with CDM. There is a general expectation by the HSE that all parties involved in a project will co-operate and co-ordinate with each other.

Key term

'Work equipment' – any machinery, appliance, apparatus or tool and any assembly of components that are used in non-domestic premises

Unit 1001 Safe working practices in construction

Find out

There are several sources for health and safety information. Use the Internet to find out more about each of the following:
- Construction Skills
- Royal Society for the Prevention of Accidents (RoSPA)
- Royal Society for the Promotion of Health (RPH).

Did you know?

Another type of on-site talk is a toolbox talk. This can be an informal meeting and cover specific issues, such as training on the use of a certain tool, or basic training. A record must be kept of everyone who attends.

Remember

As a trainee once you pass the health and safety test you will qualify for a trainee card. Once you have achieved a Level 2 qualification you can then upgrade your card to an experienced worker card. Achieving a Level 3 qualification allows you to apply for a gold card.

Figure 1.1 CSCS card

Other pieces of legislation

Legislation	Content
Reporting of Injuries, Diseases and Dangerous Occurrences Regulations 1995 (RIDDOR)	Employers have a duty to report accidents, diseases or dangerous occurrences. HSE uses this to identify where and how risks arise and to investigate serious accidents.
Control of Substances Hazardous to Health Regulations 2002 (COSHH)	State how employees and employers should work with, handle, store, transport and dispose of potentially hazardous substances. This includes substances used and generated during work (e.g. paints or dust), naturally occurring substances (e.g. sand) and biological elements (e.g. bacteria).
The Control of Noise at Work Regulations 2005	Employers must assess the risks to the employee and make sure legal limits are not exceeded, noise exposure is reduced, and hearing protection is provided along with information, instruction and training.
The Electricity at Work Regulations 1989	Cover work involving electricity. Employers must keep systems safe and regularly maintained and reduce the risk of employees coming into contact with live electrical currents.
The Manual Handling Operations Regulations 1992	Cover all work activities involving a person lifting. Manual handling should be avoided wherever possible and a risk assessment must be carried out.
The Personal Protective Equipment at Work Regulations 1992 (PPER)	PPE must be checked by a trained and competent person and must be provided by the employer free of charge with a secure storage place. Employees must know how to use PPE, the risks it will help to protect against, its purpose, how to maintain it and its limitations.
The Work at Height Regulations 2005	Employers must avoid working at height and use equipment that prevents or minimises the danger of falls. Employees must follow training, report hazards and use safety equipment.

Table 1.2 Relevant legislation

Site inductions

A site induction is the process that an individual undergoes in order to understand the potential health and safety hazards and risks they may face in their working environment. It excludes job-related skills training. Site inductions include a range of topics but will always cover operations on site, health and safety, welfare and emergency arrangements, reporting structure and the process for reporting near misses. Records must be kept showing all workers have received an induction.

Construction Skills Certification Scheme (CSCS)

The Construction Skills certification scheme requires all workers to obtain a CSCS card before working on a building site. There are various levels of cards which indicate your competence and skill background. This ensures that only skilled and safe tradespeople can work on site. To get a CSCS card all applicants must sit a health and safety test.

K2. Accident, first aid and emergency procedures and reporting

Major types of emergency

There are several major types of emergencies that could occur on site. These include not only accidents but also fires, security alerts and bomb alerts. At your site induction, it should be made perfectly clear to you what you should do in the event of an emergency.

Reporting accidents

All accidents need to be reported and recorded in the accident book and the injured person must report to a trained first aider in order to receive treatment. Serious accidents must be reported under the Reporting of Injuries, Diseases and Dangerous Occurrences Regulations 1995 (RIDDOR). The nature and seriousness of the accident will decide who it needs to be reported to. There are several types of documentation used to record accidents and emergencies.

Relevant authorised person	What to do
First aiders	All accidents must be reported to a first aider. If you are unsure who they are or cannot contact them, report it to your supervisor
Supervisors	Must be informed so they can inform the first aider and their manager, and stop the work if necessary to prevent further accidents
Safety officers	Will be alerted by your supervisor or site manager and will asses the area to check it is safe, investigate the cause of the accident and prepare a report for HSE (if needed)
HSE	Must be reported to immediately if the accident results in death or major injury and followed up by a written report within ten days. This is done on form F2508
Managers	Should be informed by the supervisor or safety officer as they may need to report to head office. They will also be tasked with contacting the HSE
Emergency services	Should be contacted as soon as possible. Usually first aiders contact ambulances and supervisors contact the fire brigade. If in doubt call the emergency services yourself

Table 1.3 Procedures for reporting an accident

Safety tip

You should also be aware of any sirens or warning noises that accompany each and every type of emergency such as bomb scares or fire alarms. Some sites may have different variations of sirens or emergency procedures, so it is vital that you pay attention and listen to all instructions. If you are unsure always ask.

Remember

Most accidents are caused by human error, which means someone has done something they shouldn't have done or, just as importantly, not done something they should have done. Accidents often happen when someone is hurrying, not paying enough attention to what they are doing or they have not received the correct training.

Remember

An accident that falls under RIDDOR should be reported by the safety officer or site manager and can be reported to the HSE by telephone (0845 300 99 23) or via the RIDDOR website. A link to this website has been made available at www.pearsonhotlinks.co.uk

The accident book

The accident book is completed by the person who had the accident or, if this is not possible, someone who is representing the injured person.

The accident book will ask for some basic details about the accident, including:

- who was involved
- what happened and where
- the date and time of the accident
- any witnesses to the accident
- the address of the injured person
- what PPE was being worn
- what first aid treatment was given.

Major and minor accidents

Often an accident will result in an injury which may be minor (for example, a cut or a bruise) or possibly major (for example, loss of a limb). Accidents can also be fatal.

Near misses

As well as reporting accidents, 'near misses' must also be reported. A 'near miss' is when an accident nearly happened but did not actually occur. Reporting near misses might identify a problem and can prevent accidents from happening in the future. This allows a company to be proactive rather than reactive.

Work-related injuries in the construction industry

Construction has the largest number of fatal injuries of all the main industry groups. In 2007−8 there were 72 fatal injuries. This gave a rate of 3.4 people injured per 100,000 workers. The rate of fatal injuries in construction over the past decade has shown a downward trend, although the rate has shown little change in the most recent years.

- From 1999−2000 to 2006−7 the rate of reported major injuries in construction fell. It is unclear whether the rise in 2007−8 means an end to this trend. Despite this falling trend, the rate of major injury in construction is the highest of any main industry group (599.2 per 100,000 employees in 2007−8).

- Compared to other industries, a higher proportion of reported injuries were caused by falls from height, falling objects and contact with moving machinery
- The THOR-GP surveillance scheme data (2006–8), indicates a higher rate of work-related illness in construction than across all industries. The rate of self-reported work-related ill health in construction is similar to other industries. (This scheme asked GPs to report work-based ill health)

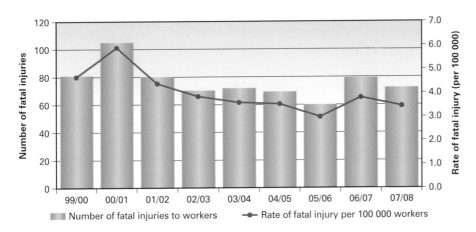

Number of fatal injuries to workers — Rate of fatal injury per 100 000 workers

Figure 1.2 Number and rate of fatal injury to workers, 1999–2000 to 2007–8

The cost of accidents

As well as the tragedy, pain and suffering that accidents cause they can also have a negative financial and business impact.

Small accidents will affect profits as sick pay may need to be paid. Production may also slow down or stop if the injured person is a specialist. Replacement or temporary workers may need to be used to keep the job going. More serious accidents will see the financial loss rise as the injured person will be off work for longer. This can cause jobs to fall seriously behind and, in extreme cases, may even cause the contractor to lose their job and possibly have to close the site.

First aid

If there are more than five people on a site, then a qualified first aider must be present at all times. On large building sites there must be several first aiders. A good first aid box should have plasters, bandages, disposable gloves, eye patches, slings, wound dressings and safety pins. Other equipment, such as eye wash stations, must also be available if the work being carried out requires it.

Figure 1.3 A first aid box provides the supplies to deal with minor injuries

Actions for an unsafe area

On discovering an accident the first thing to do is to ensure that the victim is in no further danger. This will require you to do tasks such as switching off the electricity supply. Tasks like this must only be done if there is no danger to yourself. You should then contact the first aider or emergency services for help.

K3. Hazards on construction sites

A major part of health and safety at work is being able to identify hazards and to help prevent them in the first place, therefore avoiding the risk of injury.

Hazards on the building site

The building industry can be a very dangerous place to work and there are certain hazards that all workers need to be aware of. Some of these common hazards are covered later in this unit: falling from height (page 15), electrical (page 16) and fires (page 19).

Hazard	What to do
Tripping	Caused by poor **housekeeping**. Keep workplaces tidy and debris free.
Chemical spills	Most are small with minimal risk and can be easily cleaned. If the spill is hazardous, take the correct action promptly. To do this you must be familiar with the qualities of the particular chemical you are working with.
Burns	From fires or chemical materials. You must be aware of the dangers and take the correct precautions.

Table 1.4 Common hazards

Risk assessments

You will have noticed that most of the legislation we have looked at requires **risk assessments** to be carried out. The Management of Health and Safety at Work Regulations 1999 requires every employer to make suitable and sufficient assessment of:

- the risks to the health and safety of their employees to which the employees are exposed while at work
- the risks to the health and safety of persons not in their employment arising out of or in connection with their work activities.

Figure 1.4 An untidy work site can present many hazards

It is vital that you know how to carry out a risk assessment. Often you may be in a position where you are given direct responsibility for this, and the care and attention you take over it may have a direct impact on the safety of others. You must be aware of the dangers or hazards of any task, and know what can be done to prevent or reduce the risk.

There are five steps in a risk assessment.

Step 1 Identify the hazards.

Step 2 Identify who is at risk.

Step 3 Calculate the risk from the hazard against the likelihood of it taking place.

Step 4 Introduce measures to reduce the risk.

Step 5 Monitor the risk.

Method statements

A method statement is a key safety document that takes the information about significant risks from your risk assessment, and combines it with the job specification, to produce a practical and safe working method for the workers to follow for tasks on site.

Hazard books

The hazard book is a tool used on some sites that identifies hazards within certain tasks and can help to produce risk assessments. The book will list tasks and what hazards are associated with those tasks.

K4. Health and hygiene

One of the easiest ways to stay healthy is to wash your hands on a regular basis to prevent hazardous substances, such as the bacteria that causes **leptospirosis**, from entering your body. You should always clean any cuts you may get to prevent infection. Welfare facilities should be provided for employees. These include toilets, washing facilities, drinking water, storage and lunch areas.

Substance abuse

This covers things such as drinking alcohol and taking drugs. Taking drugs at work is not only illegal but highly dangerous as it can effect your concentration. Drinking alcohol can also slow your reflexes and reduce your concentration.

Remember

There may be different hazards that are associated with tasks. Different working environments can create different types of hazard so risk assessments must always look at the specific task and not a generic one. For example, when a hazardous substance is being used, a COSHH or risk assessment will have been made, and it should include a plan for dealing with a spillage.

Functional skills

When completing risk assessments you will be practising the following functional skills: **FE 1.3.1 – 1.3.5**: Write clearly with a level of detail to suit the purpose.

Figure 1.5 Wash your hands regularly

Key term

Leptospirosis – an infectious disease that affects humans and animals causing fever, muscle pain and jaundice. In severe cases it can affect the liver and kidneys. It is spread by infected urine and can be caught from contaminated soil or water. The human form is commonly called Weil's disease.

Did you know?

Noise is measured in decibels (dB). The average person may notice a rise of 3dB, but with every 3dB rise, the noise is doubled. What may seem like a small rise is actually very significant.

Health effects of noise

Damage to hearing can be caused by one of two things:

- **intensity** – you can be hurt in an instant from an explosive or very loud noise which can burst your ear drum
- **duration** – noise doesn't have to be deafening to harm you, it can be a quieter noise over a long period, for example a 12- hour shift.

Hazardous substances

Hazardous substances are a major health and safety risk on a construction site. They must be handled, stored, transported and disposed of in very specific ways.

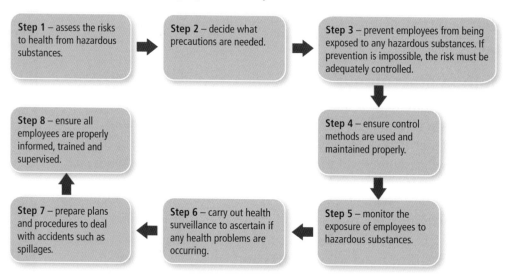

Step 1 – assess the risks to health from hazardous substances.

Step 2 – decide what precautions are needed.

Step 3 – prevent employees from being exposed to any hazardous substances. If prevention is impossible, the risk must be adequately controlled.

Step 4 – ensure control methods are used and maintained properly.

Step 5 – monitor the exposure of employees to hazardous substances.

Step 6 – carry out health surveillance to ascertain if any health problems are occurring.

Step 7 – prepare plans and procedures to deal with accidents such as spillages.

Step 8 – ensure all employees are properly informed, trained and supervised.

Figure 1.6 Process for dealing with hazardous substances

Ask the supplier or manufacturer for a COSHH data sheet, outlining the risks involved with a substance. Most substance containers carry a warning sign stating whether the contents are corrosive, harmful, toxic or bad for the environment. Exposure to chemicals can cause skin problems.

a   b   c

Key term

Dermatitis – a skin condition where the affected area is red, itchy and sore

Figure 1.7 Common safety signs for corrosive (a), toxic (b) and explosive (c) materials

Adhesives

Adhesives are used to bond (stick) surfaces together and should all be stored and used in line with manufacturer's instructions. Usually, these are to store on shelves, with labels facing outwards, in a safe, secure area (preferably a lockable store room). It is important to keep the labels facing outwards so that the correct adhesive can be selected.

Paint and decorating materials

Type	Storage issues
Oil- and water-based	Store at a constant temperature in date order (new stock at the back) on clearly marked shelves with the labels turned to the front. Regularly **invert** to prevent settlement or separation of ingredients and keep tightly sealed to prevent **skinning**. Water-based paints should be protected from frost to prevent freezing.
Powdered materials	Heavy bags should be stored at ground level. Smaller items should be stored on shelves with loose materials in sealed containers. Protect from frost, moisture and high humidity.
Hazardous materials	Some materials have **volatile** or highly flammable characteristics, including spirits (i.e. methylated or white), turpentine (turps), paint thinners and varnish removers. Store out of the way on shelves in a suitable locker or room that meets COSHH requirements. The temperature must be kept below 15°C to prevent explosions.

Table 1.7 How to store paint and decorating materials

K6. Basic working platforms

Fall protection

Working at height will be covered in depth in Unit 2024 (pages 251–66). With any task involving working at height, the main danger is falling. There are certain tasks where edge protection or scaffolding simply cannot be used. In these instances some form of fall protection must be used. There is also the danger of objects falling from height and striking workers and people below. Barriers should be used to prevent this.

Type of fall protection	Description
Harnesses and lanyards	Harness is attached to the worker and a lanyard to a secure beam/eyebolt. If the worker slips, they will fall only the length of the lanyard.
Safety netting	Used on the top floor where there is no point for a lanyard. Nets are attached to the joists to catch any falling workers.
Airbags	Made from interlinked modular air mattresses that expand together to form a soft fall surface. System must be kept inflated. Ideal for short fall jobs, but should not be used for long fall jobs.

Table 1.8 Fall protection systems

Figure 1.8 Correct storage of paints

Figure 1.9 A harness and lanyard can prevent a worker from falling to the ground

> **Key terms**
>
> **Invert** – tip and turn upside down
>
> **Skinning** – the formation of a skin which occurs when the top layer dries out
>
> **Volatile** – quick to evaporate (turn to a gas)

K7. Working with electricity

Electricity is a killer. One of the main problems with electricity is that it is invisible. You don't even have to be working with an electric tool to be electrocuted. You can get an electric shock when you are:

- working too close to live overhead cables
- plastering a wall with electric sockets
- carrying out maintenance work on a floor
- drilling into a wall.

Voltages

There are two main types of voltage in use in the UK. These are 230 V and 110 V. The standard UK power supply is 230 V and this is what all the sockets in your house are.

It is unsafe to use 230 V on construction sites so 110 V must be used here. The 110 V supply is identified by a yellow and different style plug. It works from a transformer which converts the 230 V to 110 V.

When working within domestic dwellings where 230V is the standard power source ideally a portable transformer should be used. If this is not possible then residual current devices (RCD) should be used.

Contained within the wiring there should be three wires: the live and neutral, which carry the alternating current, and the earth wire, which acts as a safety device. The three wires are colour-coded as follows to make them easy to recognise:

- Live – Brown
- Neutral – Blue
- Earth – Yellow and green.

Dealing with electric shocks

The best way to deal with electric shocks is to take precautions to prevent them. You will find advice on handling power tools safely on page 13.

Figure 1.11 A 110 V plug

Did you know?

Around 30 workers die from electricity-related accidents every year, with over 1000 more being seriously injured (source: HSE).

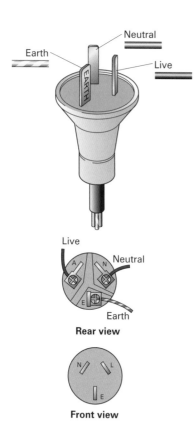

Figure 1.10 Colour coding of the wires in a 110 V plug

Safety tip

The colour coding of the wires has been changed recently to comply with European colours. Some older properties will have the following colours:
Live – Red
Neutral – Black
Earth – Yellow and green.

Skin and sun protection

Another precaution you can take is ensuring that you wear barrier cream. This is a cream used to protect the skin from damage and infection. Don't forget to ensure that your skin is protected from the sun with a good sunscreen, and make sure your back, arms and legs are covered by suitable clothing.

Whole body protection

The rest of the body also needs protecting when working on site. This will usually involve either overalls, which protect from dirt and minor cuts, or high-visibility jackets which make the wearer visible at all times.

K9. Fire and emergency procedures

Fires can start almost anywhere and at any time, but a fire needs all the ingredients of 'the triangle of fire' to burn. Remove one side of the triangle, and the fire will be extinguished. Fire moves by consuming all these ingredients and burns fuel as it moves.

Fires can be classified according to the type of material that is involved:

- **Class A** – wood, paper, textiles, etc.
- **Class B** – flammable liquids, petrol, oil, etc.
- **Class C** – flammable gases, liquefied petroleum gas (LPG), propane, etc.
- **Class D** – metal, metal powder, etc.
- **Class E** – electrical equipment.

Fire fighting equipment

There are several types of fire fighting equipment, such as fire blankets, fire extinguishers and fire blankets. Each type is designed to be the most effective at putting out a particular class of fire and some should never be used in certain types of fire.

Fire extinguishers

A fire extinguisher is a metal canister containing a substance that can put out a fire. There are several different types and it is important that you learn which type should be used on specific classes of fires.

Figure 1.18 A respiratory system

Figure 1.19 Safety gloves

Figure 1.20 The triangle of fire

Find out

What fire risks are there in the construction industry? Think about some of the materials (fuel) and heat sources that could make up two sides of 'the triangle of fire'.

Remember

- Remove the fuel – without anything to burn, the fire will go out.
- Remove the heat and the fire will go out.
- Remove the oxygen and the fire will go out – without oxygen, a fire won't even ignite.

Fire extinguisher	Colour Band	Main use	Details
Water fire extinguisher	Red	Class A fires	Never use this for an electrical or burning fat/oil fire, as water can conduct the electricity back to the person using the extinguisher. Putting water on oil or fat fires will 'explode' the fire, making it worse.
Foam fire extinguisher	Cream	Class A fires	This can also be used on Class B if no liquid is flowing and on Class C if gas is in liquid form.
Carbon dioxide (CO$_2$) extinguisher	Black	Class E	Primarily used on electrical fires, can also be used in Class A, B and C.
Dry powder extinguisher	Blue	All classes	Most commonly used on electrical and liquid fires. The powder puts out the fire by smothering the flames.

Table 1.9 Fire extinguishers and their uses

Fire blankets

Fire blankets are made of a fireproof material and work by smothering the fire and stopping any more oxygen from getting to it, thus putting it out. A fire blanket can also be used if a person is on fire.

Safety tip

It is important to remember that when you put out a fire with a fire blanket, you must take extra care as you will have to get quite close to the fire.

Figure 1.21 A fire blanket

What to do in the event of a fire

During your induction to any workplace, you will be made aware of the fire procedure as well as where the fire assembly points (also known as muster points) are and what the alarm sounds like. All muster points should be clearly indicated by signs, and a map of their location clearly displayed in the building. On hearing the alarm you must stop what you are doing and make your way calmly to the nearest muster point. This is so that everyone can be accounted for. If you do not go to the muster point, or if you leave before someone has taken your name, someone may risk their life to go back into the fire to get you.

> **Remember**
> Fire and smoke can kill in seconds, so think and act clearly, quickly and sensibly.

K10. Safety signs and notices

There are many different safety signs but each will usually fit into one of four categories:

- **Prohibition signs** – these tell you that something **MUST NOT** be done. They always have a white background and a red circle with a red line through it.
- **Mandatory signs** – these tell you that something **MUST** be done. They are also circular, but have a white symbol on a blue background.
- **Warning signs** – these signs are there to alert you to a specific hazard. They are triangular and have a yellow background and a black border.
- **Safe condition signs** (often called information signs) – these give you useful information such as the location of things (for example, a first aid point). They can be square or rectangular and are green with a white symbol.

Figure 1.22 A Prohibition sign

Figure 1.23 A Mandatory sign

Figure 1.24 A Warning sign

First Aid box

Figure 1.25 A Safe condition sign

FAQ

When do I need to do a risk assessment?

A risk assessment should be carried out if there is any chance of an accident happening as a direct result of the work being done. To be on the safe side, you should make a risk assessment before starting each task.

Do I need to read and understand every regulation?

No. It is part of your employer's duty to ensure that you are aware of what you need to know.

What determines the type of scaffolding used on a job?

Only a carded scaffolder is allowed to erect or alter scaffolding. They will select the scaffolding to be used according to the ground condition of the site, whether or not people will be working on the scaffolding, the types of material and equipment that will be used on the scaffolding and the height to which the access will be needed.

What happens if there is a delivery of timber but there is no room in the wood store?

It is probably best to remove some of the old stock from the wood store and either store it flat on timber cross-bearers or on edge in racks. This timber should be used first and as soon as possible. The new timber can now be stored in the wood store.

What should I do if I notice a leakage in the LPG store?

Leaking LPG should be treated as a very dangerous situation. Don't turn on any lights or ignite any naked flames, for example cigarette lighters. Any kind of spark could ignite the LPG. Report the situation immediately and don't attempt to clear up the spillage yourself.

Check it out

1. What do COSHH and RIDDOR stand for?
2. Describe what might happen to you or your employer if a health and safety law is broken.
3. Write a method statement stating the actions you can take to avoid injury when lifting and carrying loads using manual handling techniques.
4. Describe the class(es) of fire that can be put out with a carbon dioxide (CO_2) extinguisher.
5. Describe why it is important to report 'near misses'.
6. State two sources of health and safety information and give a small explanation of what services they provide.
7. Prepare a method statement, describing what should be covered during a site induction.
8. State why the CSCS scheme was introduced.
9. Write a method statement explaining the process that should be followed in the event of a fire.
10. Explain why you may see the different safety signs, with examples of the use of each.

Getting ready for assessment

The information contained in this unit, as well as continued health and safety good practice throughout your training, will help you with preparing for both your end-of-unit test and the diploma multiple-choice test. It will also help you to understand the dangers of working in the construction industry. Wherever you work in the construction industry, you will need to understand the dangers you are likely to encounter. You will also need to know the safe working practices for the work required for your synoptic practical assignments.

Your college or training centre should provide you with the opportunity to practise these skills, as part of preparing for the test.

You will need to know about and understand:

- the safety rules and regulations
- accident and emergency procedures
- how to identify hazards on site
- health and hygiene
- safe handling of materials and equipment
- working at heights
- working with electricity
- using personal protective equipment (PPE)
- fire and emergency procedures
- safety signs.

You will need to apply the things you have learned in this unit to the actual work you will be carrying out in the synoptic test, and in your professional life. For example, with learning outcome two you will need to know how to perform emergency evacuation procedures and locate first aid equipment for any emergencies. You will need to demonstrate how to report accidents and emergencies to authorised persons. This will include first aiders, supervisors, safety officers, the HSE, managers and emergency services. As part of this you will need to be able to complete accident and emergency records, including the accident book, first aid records and other documentation. To promote health and safety you will need to be able to analyse national statistics for key accident trends within the UK construction industry.

Before you start work you should always think of a plan of action. You will need to know the clear sequences that materials for the practical are to be constructed in to be sure you are not making mistakes as you work and that you are working safely at all times.

Your speed in carrying out these tasks in a practice setting will also help to prepare you for the time set for the test. However you must never rush the test! This is particularly important with health and safety, as you must always make sure you are working safely. Make sure throughout the test that you are wearing appropriate and correct PPE and using tools correctly.

This unit has explained the dangers you may face when working. Understanding these dangers, and the precautions that can be taken to help prevent them, will not only aid you in your training but will help you remain safe and healthy throughout your working life.

Good luck!

CHECK YOUR KNOWLEDGE

1 A risk assessment should be done:

  a when the job involves more than 50 people

  b for every job

  c never

  d only when working on a scaffold

2 Leptospirosis is also known as:

  a Weil's disease

  b dermatitis

  c vibration white finger

  d none of the above

3 The most common injury from incorrect manual handling is:

  a broken fingernails

  b spinal injury

  c crushing fingers under the item being handled

  d dropping the item being handled onto toes

4 With regards to PPE, what must your employer do?

  a supply you with it

  b not charge you for it

  c ensure you wear it

  d do all of the above

5 What is the first thing to do if you suspect a co-worker is having an electric shock?

  a move them away from the power source

  b Switch off the power

  c dial 999

  d start first aid procedure

6 With regards to PPE, the employee must:

  a not misuse it

  b wear it when needed.

  c report any damage to it

  d do all of the above

7 A fire extinguisher with a red coloured band can be used on:

  a class A fires

  b class B fires

  c class C fires

  d class D fires

8 Under RIDDOR your employer must report:

  a near misses

  b any accident that results in the loss of three consecutive work days

  c cut fingers

  d all of the above

9 When lifting manually you should:

  a have your feet shoulder-width apart

  b have your back slightly bent

  c keep the load away from your body

  d lift using your back muscles

10 Which of the following can be the cause of an electric shock?

  a working too close to electric power lines

  b drilling into an internal brick/block wall

  c plastering walls with electric sockets

  d all of the above

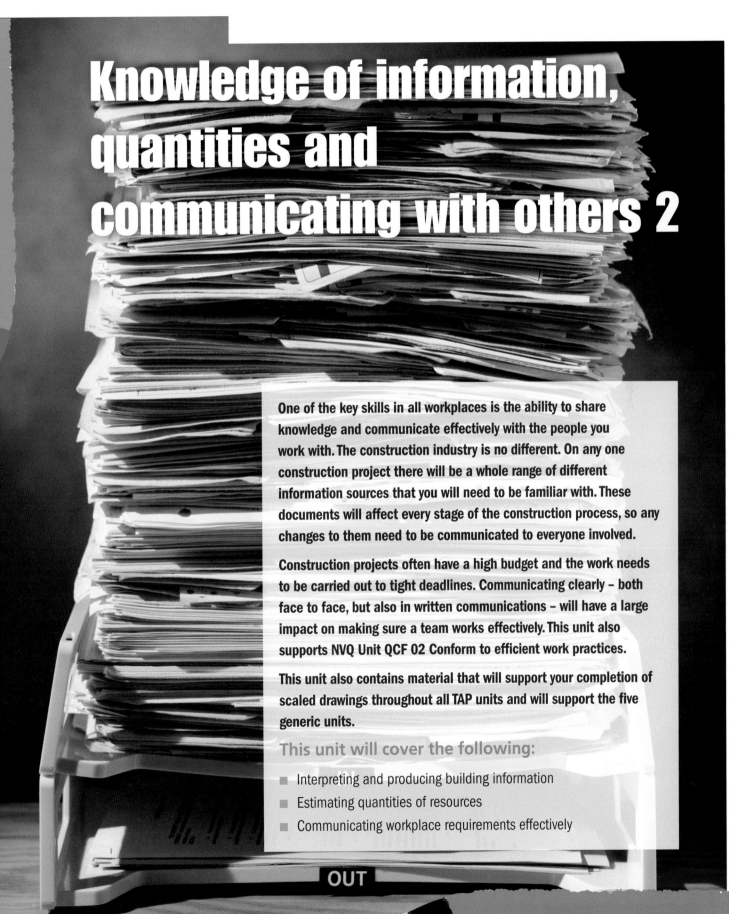

Knowledge of information, quantities and communicating with others 2

One of the key skills in all workplaces is the ability to share knowledge and communicate effectively with the people you work with. The construction industry is no different. On any one construction project there will be a whole range of different information sources that you will need to be familiar with. These documents will affect every stage of the construction process, so any changes to them need to be communicated to everyone involved.

Construction projects often have a high budget and the work needs to be carried out to tight deadlines. Communicating clearly – both face to face, but also in written communications – will have a large impact on making sure a team works effectively. This unit also supports NVQ Unit QCF 02 Conform to efficient work practices.

This unit also contains material that will support your completion of scaled drawings throughout all TAP units and will support the five generic units.

This unit will cover the following:

■ Interpreting and producing building information
■ Estimating quantities of resources
■ Communicating workplace requirements effectively

Functional skills

To store materials safely and correctly, you will need to be familiar with the manufacturer's instructions. In doing this you will be practising **FE 1.2.3:** Reading different texts and taking appropriate action

K1. Interpreting and producing building information

There are a number of types of information available. You will be familiar with these from Level 1. The most commonly used are discussed below.

Drawings

Drawings are done by the architect and are used to pass on the client's wishes to the building contractor. Drawings are usually done to scale because it would be impossible to draw a full-sized version of the project. A common scale is 1:10, which means that a line 10 mm long on the drawing represents 100 mm in real life. Drawings often contain symbols instead of written words to get the maximum amount of information across without cluttering the page. They are covered in more detail on page 33.

Hierarchical charts

This chart shows the level of authority and reporting lines for all people working on site, from the top (most authority) to the bottom (least authority).

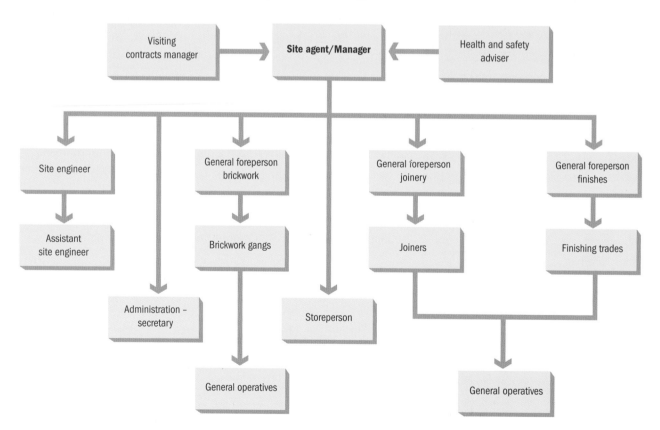

Figure 2.1 A hierarchical chart

Work programmes

Work programmes are a method of showing very easily what work is being carried out when. The most common form of work programme is a bar chart, listing tasks down the left side and a timeline across the top.

Procedures

Procedures are the ways in which a company will go about doing certain tasks. Larger companies will have procedures for most things, including ordering materials, making payments, etc.

Mediation

Mediation occurs after a conflict arises between two or more groups who can't agree on an outcome. A mediator is installed to listen to all sides of the debate and try to resolve the conflict by making compromises and changes so that all parties agree.

Mediators can come from outside organisations. It is important that mediators are not seen to have any stake in the outcome of the solution. If they did, then it could influence the decision that they reach.

Before a mediation, both sides often agree to abide with the final decision of the mediator.

Disciplinary

A disciplinary is what employees receive for breaches in company rules. A disciplinary can either be verbal or written, with serious offences leading to sacking.

The type of disciplinary procedure used will depend on the offence. Most companies will run a 'three strike system' wherein you will receive three warnings before you are sacked.

Serious breaches such as theft or violence may result in the employee being suspended until an investigation has been carried out. If the findings state the employee has done what they are accused of then it will lead to instant dismissal.

Manufacturer's technical information

Everything you buy, whether it is a power tool or a bag of cement, will always come with the manufacturer's technical information. This information will list how the component should be used and what its capabilities are.

Remember

It is important to follow the procedures your company uses, as this is the easiest way of ensuring that everyone you work with will understand what you have done and why.

Did you know?

Organisations are required by law to give at least one written warning before dismissing an employee. However, most employees have clauses in their contract stating that they can be dismissed instantly for a serious breach.

Remember

Reading the technical information from the manufacturers will not only give you useful information about how to use the product, it will also allow you to confirm that it is right for the job for which you are planning to use it.

Power tools often have their technical information provided in a booklet, which will give you detailed instructions on how the machine is set up, used and so forth.

Bagged materials, such as cement, will normally have information on the bag. Even lengths of timber will have technical information, but for this you may need to contact the manufacturer. With lengths of timber this is important as timber is strength graded and you need to be sure that the materials you are planning to use are up to the job.

Organisation documentation

No building site functions without paperwork. Some of the key documents include:

- **Day worksheets** – often confused with time sheets, but different as they are used when there is no price or estimate for the work, to enable the contractor to charge. They record work done, hours worked and materials used.
- **Time sheets** – these record hours worked and are completed by every employee individually. They can be used to work out how many hours the client will be charged for.
- **Job sheets** – these are used when the work has already been priced and enable the worker to see what needs to be done and the site agent to see what has been completed.
- **Variation orders** – these are used by the architect to make any changes to the original plans, including omissions, alterations and extra works.

P. Gresford Building Contractors

Day worksheet

Customer Chris MacFarlane Date

Description of work being carried out

Hang internal door in kitchen.

Labour	Craft	Hours	Gross rate	TOTALS
Materials	Quantity	Rate	% addition	
Plant	Hours	Rate	% addition	

Comments

Signed Date

Site manager/foreman signature

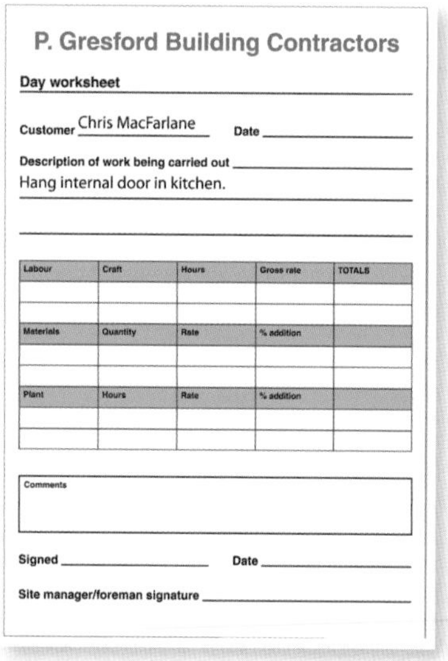

Figure 2.2 A day worksheet

P. Gresford Building Contractors

Timesheet

Employee Project/site

Date	Job no.	Start time	Finish time	Total time	Travel time	Expenses
M						
Tu						
W						
Th						
F						
Sa						
Su						
Totals						

Employee's signature

Supervisor's signature

Date

Figure 2.3 A time sheet

P. Gresford Building Contractors

Job sheet

Customer Chris MacFarlane

Address 1 High Street
Any Town
Any County

Work to be carried out

Hang internal door in kitchen

Special conditions/instructions

Fit with door closer
3 × 75mm butt hinges

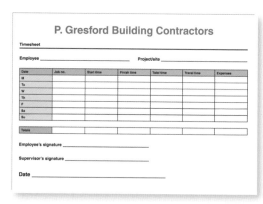

Figure 2.4 A job sheet

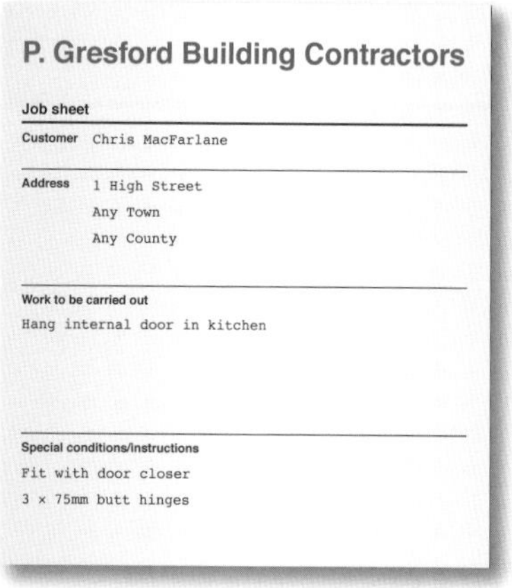

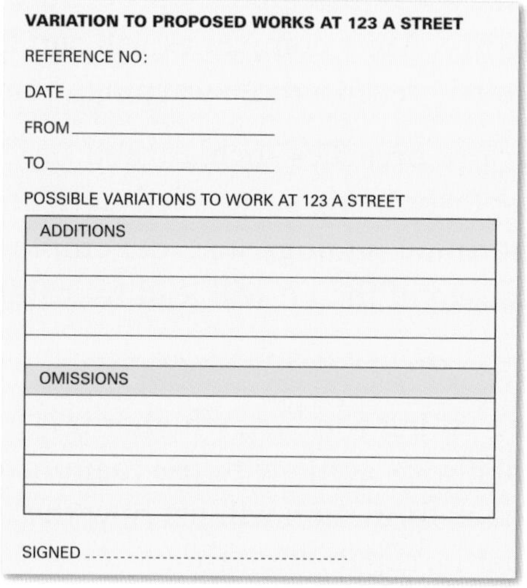

VARIATION TO PROPOSED WORKS AT 123 A STREET

REFERENCE NO:

DATE

FROM

TO

POSSIBLE VARIATIONS TO WORK AT 123 A STREET

ADDITIONS

OMISSIONS

SIGNED

Figure 2.5 A variation order

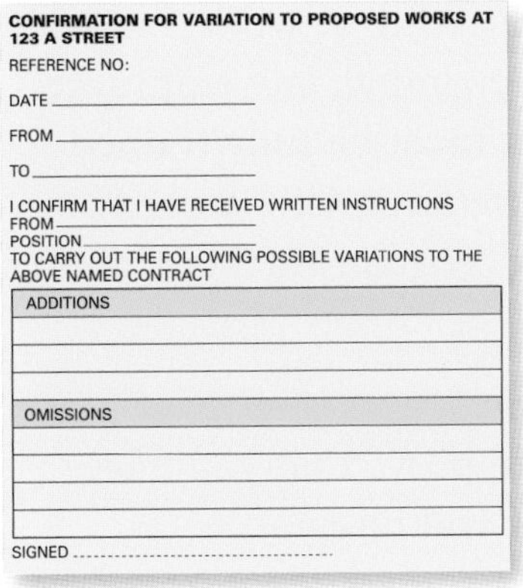

CONFIRMATION FOR VARIATION TO PROPOSED WORKS AT 123 A STREET
REFERENCE NO:
DATE
FROM
TO
I CONFIRM THAT I HAVE RECEIVED WRITTEN INSTRUCTIONS
FROM
POSITION
TO CARRY OUT THE FOLLOWING POSSIBLE VARIATIONS TO THE ABOVE NAMED CONTRACT

ADDITIONS
OMISSIONS

SIGNED

Figure 2.6 A confirmation notice

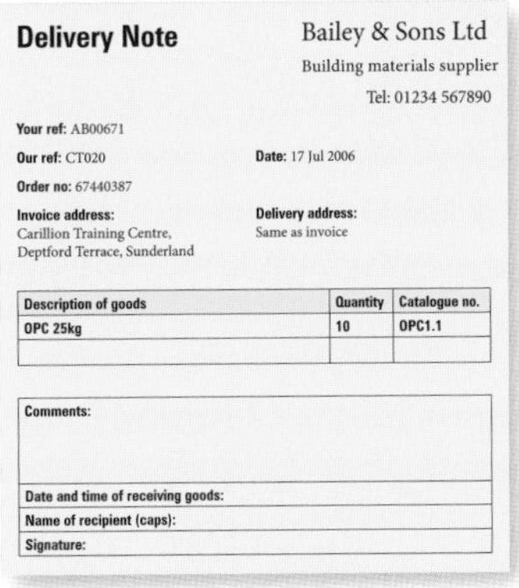

Delivery Note

Bailey & Sons Ltd
Building materials supplier
Tel: 01234 567890

Your ref: AB00671
Our ref: CT020 Date: 17 Jul 2006
Order no: 67440387
Invoice address: Carillion Training Centre, Deptford Terrace, Sunderland
Delivery address: Same as invoice

Description of goods	Quantity	Catalogue no.
OPC 25kg	10	OPC1.1

Comments:
Date and time of receiving goods:
Name of recipient (caps):
Signature:

Figure 2.7 A delivery note

INVOICE

JARVIS BUILDING SUPPLIES
3rd AVENUE
THOMASTOWN

L Weeks Builders
4th Grove
Thomastown

Quantity	Description	Unit price	Vat rate	Total
30	Galvanised joist hangers	£1.32	20%	£47.52
			TOTAL	£47.52

To be paid within 30 days from receipt of this invoice
Please direct any queries to 01234 56789

Figure 2.8 An invoice

- **Confirmation notices** – given to the contractor to confirm any changes made in the variation order, so that the contractor can go ahead.
- **Orders/requisitions** – used to order materials from a supplier.
- **Delivery notes** – given to the contractor by the supplier, listing all the materials and components being delivered. Each should be checked for accuracy against the order and the delivery (to ensure that what is delivered is correct and matches the note).
- **Invoices** – these come from a variety of sources and state what services or goods have been provided and the charge for them.
- **Delivery records** – these list all deliveries over a certain period (usually a month) and are sent to the contractor's head office so that payment can be made.
- **Daily reports** – used to pass general information on to a company's head office.
- **Accident** and **near-miss reports** – it is a legal requirement that a company has an accident book in which all reports must be made. Reports must also be made when an accident nearly happened but did not occur – a 'near miss'.

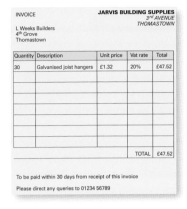

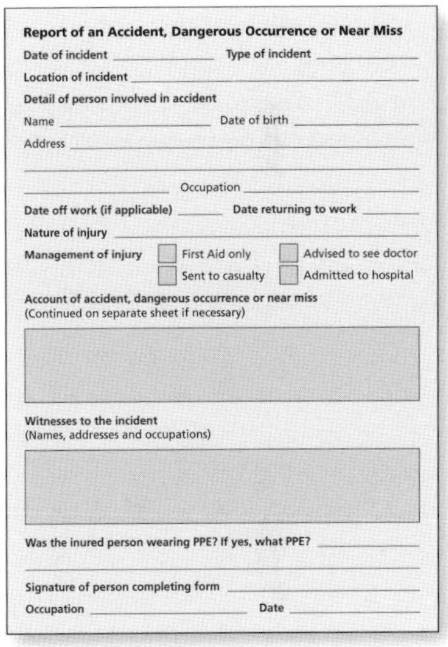

Report of an Accident, Dangerous Occurrence or Near Miss
Date of incident Type of incident
Location of incident
Detail of person involved in accident
Name Date of birth
Address
Occupation
Date off work (if applicable) Date returning to work
Nature of injury
Management of injury ☐ First Aid only ☐ Advised to see doctor ☐ Sent to casualty ☐ Admitted to hospital
Account of accident, dangerous occurrence or near miss (Continued on separate sheet if necessary)
Witnesses to the incident (Names, addresses and occupations)
Was the inured person wearing PPE? If yes, what PPE?
Signature of person completing form
Occupation Date

Figure 2.9 An accident/near-miss report

Training and development records

As learners in the construction industry you are currently undertaking training that will develop your skills. During your training there will be records of what you have been trained in. These are used at the end of your training as evidence so that you can achieve your qualification.

However, training doesn't stop as soon as you qualify! Further training and development is important in the construction industry, especially with technological advances in tools, methods of working and other changes to the industry.

Did you know?

Larger companies, and even some small ones, may see the potential of certain employees and will try to develop them through training. For example, a worker may be sent on a supervisor training course.

It is this development that allows companies to promote from within rather than to advertise for external candidates. The next site managers need to come from somewhere!

Key term

Conformity – following a fixed standard, regulation or requirement

There will be certain tasks you are introduced to at work that will require you to receive some training. For example, any employee who intends to use tools such as nail guns must be fully trained in their functions before they can use them. Even CSCS card holders and/or experienced personnel may require further training and development.

Records of all training and certficates issued must be kept, as if you leave one employer you may need to prove that you have received training before another employer will hire you.

Checking information for conformity

As with all documents, the information above needs to be checked for **conformity**. Using documents that don't conform to, or meet, the company's standards could cause problems, delays or confusion in the building process. For example, faxing a blank piece of paper with a few materials listed on it to a supplier may be rejected by the supplier which will lead to materials not being ordered and delays to the build.

Only documents that have been approved must be used. If in doubt ask your supervisor.

Contract documents and interpreting specifications

Contract documents are also vital to a construction project. They are created by a team of specialists – the architect, structural engineer, services engineer and quantity surveyor – who first look at the draft of drawings from the architect and client.
Just which contract documents this team goes on to produce will vary depending on the size and type of work being done, but will usually include:

- plans and drawings
- specification
- schedules
- bill of quantities
- conditions of contract.

Plans and drawings are covered in detail on page 33.

Specification

The specification or 'spec' is a document produced alongside the plans and drawings and is used to show information that cannot be shown on the drawings. Specifications are almost always used for things such as:

- foundations
- walls
- materials
- surface finishes
- floors
- roofs
- components.

The only exceptions might be in the case of very small contracts. A specification should contain:

- **site description** – a brief description of the site including the address
- **restrictions** – what restrictions apply, such as working hours or limited access
- **services** – what services are available, what services need to be connected and what type of connection should be used
- **materials description** – including type, sizes, quality, moisture content, etc.
- **workmanship** – including methods of fixing, quality of work and finish.

The specification may also name subcontractors or suppliers, or give details such as how the site should be cleared, and so on.

Figure 2.10 A good 'spec' helps avoid confusion when dealing with subcontractors or suppliers

Schedules

A schedule is used to record repeated design information that applies to a range of components or fittings. Schedules are mainly used on bigger sites where there are multiples of several types of house (4-bedroom, 3-bedroom, 3-bedroom with dormers, etc.), each type having different components and fittings. The schedule avoids the wrong component or fitting being put in the wrong house. Schedules can also be used on smaller jobs such as a block of flats with 200 windows, where there are six different types of window.

Figure 2.11 Every item needed should be listed on the bill of quantities

Bill of quantities

The bill of quantities is produced by the quantity surveyor. It gives a complete description of everything that is required to do the job, including labour, materials and any items or components, based on information from the drawings, specification and schedule. The same bill of quantities is sent out to all prospective contractors so they can submit a tender based on the same information – this helps the client select the best contractor for the job.

Item ref No	Description	Quantity	Unit	Rate £	Cost £
A1	Treated 50 × 225mm sawn carcass	200	M		
A2	Treated 75 × 225mm sawn carcass	50	M		
B1	50mm galvanised steel joist hangers	20	N/A		
B2	75mm galvanised steel joist hangers	7	N/A		
C1	Supply and fit the above floor joists as described in the preambles				

Figure 2.12 Extract from a bill of quantities

All bills of quantities contain the following information:

- **preliminaries** – general information such as the names of the client and architect, details of the work and descriptions of the site
- **preambles** – similar to the specification, outlining the quality and description of materials and workmanship.
- **measured quantities** – a description of how each task or material is measured with measurements in metres (linear and square), hours, litres, kilograms or simply the number of components required
- **provisional quantities** – approximate amounts where items or components cannot be measured accurately
- **cost** – the amount of money that will be charged per unit of quantity.

The bill of quantities may also contain:

- any costs that may result from using subcontractors or specialists
- a sum of money for work that has not been finally detailed
- a sum of money to cover contingencies for unforeseen work.

Figure 2.12 shows an extract from a bill of quantities that might be sent to prospective contractors, who would then complete the cost section and return it as their tender.

To ensure that all contractors interpret and understand the bill of quantities consistently, the Royal Institution of Chartered Surveyors and the Building Employers' Confederation produce a document called *Standard Method of Measurement of Building Works (SMM)*. This provides a uniform basis for measuring building work, for example stating that carcassing timber is measured by the metre whereas plasterboard is measured in square metres.

Conditions of contract

Almost all building work is carried out under a contract. A small job with a single client (for example, a loft conversion) will have a basic contract stating that the contractor will do the work to the client's satisfaction, and that the client will pay the contractor the agreed sum of money once the work is finished. Larger contracts with clients such as the government will have additional clauses, terms or stipulations, which may include any of the following.

Variations

A variation is a modification of the original drawing or specification. The architect or client must give the contractor written confirmation of the variation, then the contractor submits a price for the variation to the quantity surveyor (or client, on a small job). Once the price is accepted, the variation work can be completed.

Interim payments

An interim payment schedule may be written into the contract, meaning that the client pays for the work in instalments. The client may pay an amount each month, linked to how far the job has progressed, or may make regular payments regardless of how far the job has progressed.

Final payment

Here the client makes a one-off full payment once the job has been completed to the specification. A final payment scheme may also have additional clauses included, such as:

- **Retention** – this is when the client holds a small percentage of the full payment back for a specified period (usually six months). It may take some time for any defects to show, such as cracks in plaster. If the contractor fixes the defects, they will receive the retention payment; if they don't fix them, the retention payment can be used to hire another contractor.

- **Penalty clause** – this is usually introduced in contracts with a tight deadline, where the building must be finished and ready to operate on time. If the project overruns, the client will be unable to trade in the premises and will lose money, so the contractor will have to compensate the client for lost revenue.

Types of drawing

Working drawings

Working drawings are scaled drawings showing plans, elevations, sections, details and location of a proposed construction. They can be classified as:

- location drawings
- component range drawings
- assembly or detail drawings.

> **Did you know?**
>
> On a poorly run contract, a penalty clause can be very costly and could incur a substantial payment. In an extreme case, the contractor may end up making a loss instead of a profit on the project.

Figure 2.13 Maintaining a good relationship will keep the job running smoothly

Unit 2002 Knowledge of information, quantities and communicating with others 2

Location drawings

Location drawings give a bird's-eye view of the site. They include block plans and site plans.

Block plans identify the proposed site by giving a bird's-eye view of the site in relation to the surrounding area. An example is shown in Figure 2.14.

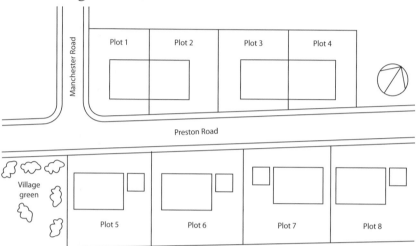

Figure 2.14 Block plan showing location

Site plans give the position of the proposed building and the general layout of the roads, services, drainage, etc. on site. An example is shown in Figure 2.15.

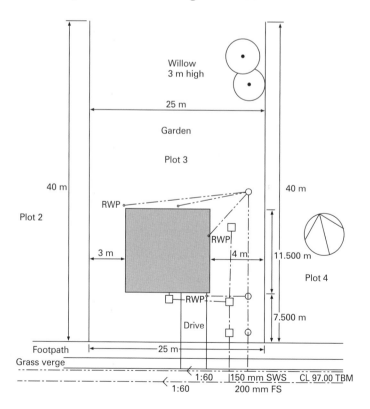

Figure 2.15 Site plan showing position (not to scale)

Component range drawings

Component range drawings show the basic sizes and reference system of a standard range of components produced by a manufacturer. This helps in selecting suitable off-the-shelf components. An example is shown in Figure 2.16.

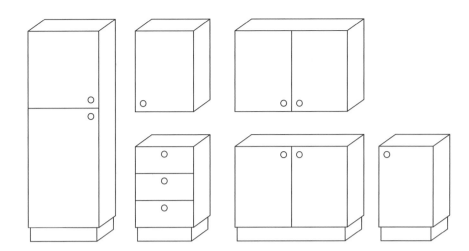

Figure 2.16 Component range drawing

Assembly or detail drawings

Assembly or detail drawings give all the information required to manufacture a given component. They show how things are put together and what the finished item will look like. An example is shown in Figure 2.17.

Types of projection

Building, engineering and similar drawings aim to give as much information as possible in a way that is easy to understand. They frequently combine several views on a single drawing.

These may be elevations (the view we would see if we stood in front or to the side of the finished building) or plans (the view we would have if we were looking down on it). The view we see depends on where we are looking from. There are then different ways of 'projecting' what we would see onto the drawings.

The two main methods of projection used on standard building drawings are orthographic and isometric.

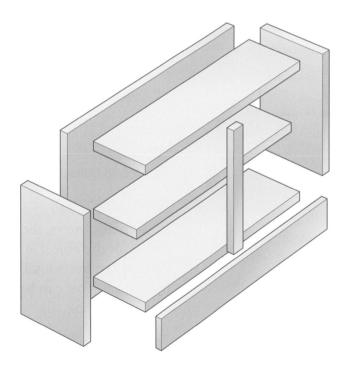

Figure 2.17 Assembly drawing

Orthographic projection

Orthographic projection works as if parallel lines were drawn from every point on a model of the building onto a sheet of paper held up behind it (an elevation view), or laid out underneath it (plan view).

There are then different ways to display the views on a drawing. The method most commonly used in the building industry for detailed construction drawings is called 'first angle projection'. In this the front elevation is roughly central. The plan view is drawn directly below the front elevation and all other elevations are drawn in line with the front elevation. An example is shown in Figure 2.18.

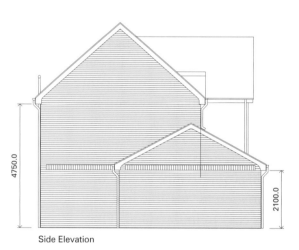

Figure 2.18 Orthographic projection

Isometric projection

In isometric views, the object is drawn at an angle where one corner of the object is closest to the viewer. Vertical lines remain vertical but horizontal lines are drawn at an angle of 30° to the horizontal. This can be seen in Figure 2.19, which shows a simple rectangular box.

Figures 2.20 and 2.21 show the method of drawing these using a T-square and set square.

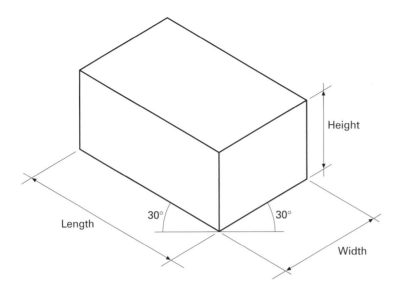

Figure 2.19 Isometric projection of a rectangular box

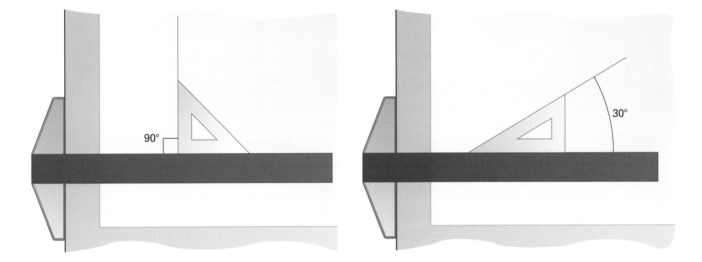

Figure 2.20 Drawing vertical lines

Figure 2.21 Drawing horizontal lines

Datum points

The need to apply levels is required at the beginning of the construction process and continues right up to the completion of building. The whole country is mapped in detail and the Ordnance Survey place datum points (bench marks) at suitable locations from which all levels can be taken.

The site datum gives a reference point on site from which all levels can be related.

> **Remember**
>
> It is important to check the date of a drawing to make sure the most up-to-date version is being used, as revisions to drawings can be frequent.

Title panels

Every drawing must have a title panel, which is normally located in the bottom right-hand corner of each drawing sheet. See Figure 2.22 for an example. The information contained in the panel is relevant to that drawing only and contains such information as:

- drawing title
- scale used
- draughtsman's name
- drawing number/project number
- company name
- job/project title
- date of drawing
- revision notes
- projection type.

ARCHITECTS	CLIENT
Peterson, Thompson Associates 237 Cumberland Way Ipswich IP3 7FT Tel: 01234 567891 Fax: 09876 543210 Email: enquiries@pta.co.uk	Carillion Development
	JOB TITLE Appleford Drive Felixstowe 4-bed detached
DRAWING TITLE Plan – garage	**SCALE:** 1:50
	DRAWING NO: 2205-06
DATE: 27.08.2010	**DRAWN BY:** RW

Figure 2.22 Typical title panel

Drawing equipment

A set of good quality drawing equipment is required when producing drawings (see figure 2.23). It should include:

Set squares

- set squares (A)
- dividers
- eraser (F)
- protractors (B)
- scale rule (D)
- drawing board (G)
- compasses (C)
- pencils (E)
- T-square (H).

Two set squares are required, one a 45° set square and the other a 60°/30° set square (not shown). These are used to draw vertical and inclined lines. A 45° set square (A) is shown in the photograph.

Protractors

Protractors (B) are used for setting out and measuring angles.

> **Did you know?**
>
> Set squares, protractors and rules should be occasionally washed in warm soapy water.

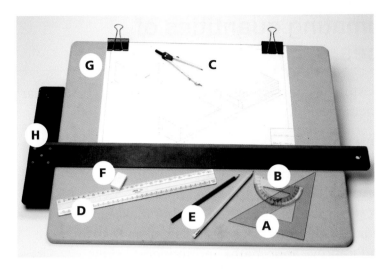

Figure 2.23 Drawing equipment

Compass and dividers

Compasses (C) are used to draw circles and arcs. Dividers (not shown) are used for transferring measurements and dividing lines.

Scale rule

A scale rule (D) that contains the following scales is to be recommended:

1:5/1:50   1:10/1:100   1:20/1:200   1:250/1:2500.

The main scales that may be used on location drawings are:

- 1:1
- 1:2
- 1:5
- 1:10
- 1:20
- 1:50.

Pencils

Two pencils (E) are required:

- HB for printing and sketching
- 2H or 3H for drawing.

Eraser

A vinyl or rubber eraser (F) is required for alterations or corrections to pencil lines.

Drawing board

A drawing board (G) is made from a smooth flat surface material, with edges truly square and parallel.

T-square

The T-square (H) is used mainly for drawing horizontal lines. Set squares are placed on the top edge of the T-square to draw vertical and inclined lines.

K2. Estimating quantities of resources

To complete estimates of calculations, you will need to be familiar with the mathematical principles behind these calculations.

Calculations

Throughout your career in the construction industry you will have to make use of numbers and calculations in order to plan and carry out work. You will therefore need to make sure you are confident dealing with numbers, which may mean that you have to develop and improve your maths and numeracy skills.

To make estimates, you will need to be familiar with some calculation techniques used in the industry. These methods will help you to calculate the amounts of materials you will need to use on a project.

Decimal numbers

Most of the time, the numbers we use are whole numbers. For example, we might buy six apples, or two loaves of bread or one car. However, sometimes we need to use numbers that are less than whole numbers, for example, we might eat one-and-a-quarter sandwiches, two-and-a-half cakes and drink three-quarters of a cup of tea. You can use decimals to show fractions or parts of quantities.

Hundreds	Tens	Units		Tenths	Hundredths	Thousandths	
		1	.	8			1.8 = 1 unit and 8 tenths 1 whole $\frac{8}{10}$
	5	6	.	4	5		56.45 = 56 and 45 hundredths $\frac{45}{100}$
2	9	0	.	0	1	7	290.017 = 290 and 17 thousandths

Table 2.1 A place value table for digits to the right of a decimal

Rounding to a number of decimal places

To round a number to a given number of decimal places, look at the digit in the place value position after the one you want.

- If it is 5 or more, round up.
- If it is less than 5, round down.

For example, to round 4.634 to 2 decimal places, the digit in the third decimal place is 4, so it is rounded down. Therefore, 4.634 rounded to 2 decimal places (d.p.) is 4.63.

Looking at the number 16.127, the digit in the third decimal place is 7, so it is rounded up. Therefore, 16.127 rounded to 2 d.p. is 16.13.

Rounding to a number of significant figures

The most significant figure in a number is the digit with the highest place value. To round a number to a given number of significant figures, look at the digit in the place value position after the one you want.

- If it is 5 or more, round up.
- If it is less than 5, round down.

For example, to write 80,597 to 1 significant figure, the most significant figure is 8. The second significant figure is 0, so it is rounded down. Therefore, 80,597 to 1 significant figure (s.f.) is 80,000.

To write 80,597 to 2 significant figures, the first 2 significant figures are 8 and 0. The third significant figure is 5, so it is rounded up. Therefore, 80,597 to 2 s.f. is 81,000.

Multiplying and dividing by 10, 100, 1000...

- To multiply a number by 10, move the digits one place value to the left.
- To multiply a number by 100, move the digits two place values to the left.
- To multiply a number by 1000, move the digits three place values to the left.

For example:

5 × 10	=	50	3.25 × 10	=	32.5
5 × 100	=	500	3.25 × 100	=	325.0
5 × 1000	=	5000	3.25 × 1000	=	3250.0

Did you know?

Knowing about place value helps you to read numbers and to put numbers and quantities in order of size.

Remember

If a calculation results in an answer with a lot of decimal places, such as 34.568923, you can round to 1 or 2 decimal places to make it simpler.

Unit 2002 Knowledge of information, quantities and communicating with others 2

> **Did you know?**
>
> Knowing how to multiply and divide by 10, 100, 1000 etc. is useful for converting metric units of measurement (see page 50) and finding percentages (see page 47).

- To divide a number by 10, move the digits one place value to the right.
- To divide a number by 100, move the digits two place values to the right.
- To divide a number by 1000, move the digits three place values to the right.

For example:

80 000 ÷ 10	= 8000	473.6 ÷ 10	=	47.36
80 000 ÷ 100	= 800	473.6 ÷ 100	=	4.736
80 000 ÷ 1000	= 80	473.6 ÷ 1000	=	0.4736

Converting decimals to fractions

You can use place value to convert a decimal to a fraction.
For example:

> **Did you know?**
>
> Knowing how to convert between fractions and decimals helps with working out parts of quantities and calculating percentages (see page 47).

0.3 is 3 tenths, which is $\dfrac{3}{10}$

0.25 is 25 hundredths, which is $\dfrac{25}{100}$

$\dfrac{25}{100}$ simplifies to $\dfrac{1}{4}$

(by dividing the top and bottom numbers by 25)

See page 44 for more on simplifying fractions.

Multiples

Multiples are the numbers you get when you multiply any number by other numbers. For example:

> **Remember**
>
> The multiples of a number are the numbers in its 'times' table (multiplication table).

- the multiples of 3 are 3, 6, 9, 12, 15, 18, 21, 24, 27, 30 and so on
- the multiples of 4 are 4, 8, 12, 16, 20, 24, 28, 32, 36, 40 and so on
- the multiples of 5 are 5, 10, 15, 20, 25, 30, 35, 40, 45, 50 and so on.

Common multiples

Here are the multiples of 3 and 5:

> **Did you know?**
>
> Knowing how to find the lowest common multiple of two numbers helps in adding and subtracting fractions (see pages 45–47).

- Multiples of 3: 3, 6, 9, 12, 15, 18, 21, 24, 27, 30, 33, 36…
- Multiples of 5: 5, 10, 15, 20, 25, 30, 35…

3 and 5 have the multiples 15 and 30 in common. 15 and 30 are common multiples of 3 and 5. The lowest common multiple of 3 and 5 is 15.

face or verbal communication. Safety signs are a good example of this and a correctly displayed safety sign will inform all who pass it of a particular issue. The downside is that not everyone passing the sign will see the information if it is poorly positioned or poorly designed. A poster or sign that is too cluttered or unclear will often just cause confusion.

Which type of communication should I use?

Of the many different types of communication, the type you should use will depend upon the situation. If someone needs to be told something formally, then written communication is generally the best way. If the message is informal, then verbal communication is usually acceptable.

The way that you communicate will also be affected by who it is you are communicating with. You should of course always communicate in a polite and respectful manner with anyone you have contact with, but you must also be aware of the need to sometimes alter the style of your communication. For example, when talking to a friend it may be fine to talk in a very informal way and use slang language, but in a work situation with a client or a colleague it is best to alter your communication to a more formal style in order to show professionalism. In the same way, it may be fine to leave a message or send a text to a friend that says 'C U @ 8 4 wk', but if you wrote this down for a work colleague or a client to read, it would not look very professional and they might not understand it.

Communication and teamwork

When working in a team communication is extremely important as you must be aware of what other members of the team are doing. This is because what you do will not only affect your working but theirs as well, and vice versa. Even simple things like lifting in a group can lead to injuries if there is no communication between the people involved – for example, one person may begin lifting when the others are not ready.

Communicating what has been done or needs to be done is also important. Duplication of labour is a big problem in teams that do not communicate well – you don't want to go and get all the materials and tools ready for a task only to discover when you get there that another member of the team has already done it. Effective communication can prevent this from happening and also help your team to work together more efficiently.

Figure 2.32 You will work with people from other trades

Communicating with other trades

Communicating with other trades is vital because they need to know what you are doing and when, and you need to know the same information from them. Poor communication can lead to delays and mistakes, and both can be costly. It is all too easy for poor communication to lead to work having to be stopped or redone. Imagine you are decorating a room in a new building. You are just about to finish when you find out that the electrician, plumber and carpenter all have work to finish in the room. This information didn't reach you and now the decorating will have to be redone once the other work has been finished. What a waste of time and money. A situation like this can be avoided with good communication between the trades.

Common methods of communicating in the construction industry

A career in construction means that you will often have to use written documents such as drawings, specifications and schedules. These documents can be very large and seem very complicated but, if you understand what they are used for and how they work, using such documents will soon become second nature.

The reasons for clear communication

Clear communication is vital for efficient relations between everyone who may be involved in a business, from the employer and employees through to clients and suppliers. You will have seen throughout this chapter that there are several different methods to ensure good communication, and that there are procedures in place to avoid major problems developing in the workplace due to unclear communication.

Most of the crucial moments when you will need to use good, clear and effective communication relate to decisions that will have a wider effect on the business and those working around you. Some examples of these include:

- **Alterations to drawings** – it is important to communicate any changes to these to everyone involved, as all the planning, estimating, material orders and work programmes will be based in part on these drawings. Not communicating changes could lead to mistakes in all these areas.

- **Variations to contracts** – the contract with the client is the crucial document that dictates all decisions that are made on a worksite. Changes to this document must be made known throughout a business.

- **Risk assessments** – the results of these assessments have a direct impact on the safety of workers on site, and should be made known to all.

- **Work restrictions** – these should be communicated to everyone as a restriction is put in place for a specific reason. The restrictions may be put in place for safety reasons. This would mean the area is unsafe so everyone who may be affected needs to be told.

Functional skills

Planning drawings for construction will give you the opportunity to practise the interpreting elements of functional skills, e.g. **FM 1.3.1:** Judge whether findings answer the original problem; **FM 1.3.2:** Communicate solutions to answer practical problems.

Working life

James is about to draw a kitchen plan for a client. Where would you begin if you were in his shoes?

Think about who to consult when planning a drawing. When talking to the client, what should James ask about? Appliances, the positioning of electrical points and the way the client intends the kitchen to be used are as important as budget and design choices.

What other considerations are there? James will need to take into account openings for doors and windows, as well as supplies for essential services like water, gas and electricity.

What other things would you include when drawing up plans?

FAQ

How many different forms are there?

A lot of forms are used in the building industry and some companies use more than others. You should ensure you get the relevant training on completing any form before using it.

How do I know what scale the drawing is at?

The scale should be written on the title panel (the box included on a plan or drawing giving basic information such as who drew it, how to contact them, the date and the scale).

How do I know if I need a schedule?

Schedules are only really used in large jobs where there is a lot of repeated design information. If your job has a lot of doors, windows, etc. it is a good idea to use one.

Check it out

1. Explain who draws up the plans for the building and their role in the construction process.
2. State three different types of drawings and give a suitable scale for each one. Draw up an example of each type of drawing you have selected.
3. State three of the main contract documents. Explain briefly what is important about each of them and the information they contain.
4. Explain the main purpose of a specification and the information it contains.
5. What is the purpose of the bill of quantities?
6. What is a penalty clause? Describe a situation where a penalty clause might be used.
7. What is a confirmation notice?
8. Why when calculating quantities of materials do you allow for wastage? Give an example of wastage on site and calculate how you might need to take this into account.
9. Name a job in each of the four construction employment areas: professional; technician; building craft worker; building operative. Prepare a brief job description for the job you have selected.
10. Explain why the client is the most important member of the building team.

Getting ready for assessment

The information contained in this unit, as well as continued practical assignments that you will carry out in your college or training centre, will help you with preparing for both your end-of-unit test and the diploma multiple-choice test. It will also aid you in preparing for the work that is required for the synoptic practical assignments.

Working with contract documents such as drawings, specifications and schedules is something that you will be required to do within your Apprenticeship and even more so after you have qualified.

You will need to know about and be familiar with:
- interpreting building information
- determining quantities of material
- relaying information in the workplace.

To get all the information you need out of these documents you will need to build on the maths and arithmetic skills that you learned at school. These skills will give you the understanding and knowledge you will need to complete many of the practical assignments, which will require you to carry out calculations and measurements.

You will also need to use your English and reading skills. These skills will be particularly important, as you will need to make sure that you are following all the details of any instructions you receive. This will be the same for the instructions you receive for the synoptic test, as it will for any specifications you might use in your professional life.

Communication skills have been a particular focus of this unit, and of learning outcome three. This unit has shown who the key personnel involved in the communication cycle are and demonstrated how poor communication between these people can have a bad effect on business and teamwork. You will need to be sure that you follow these guidelines for clear communication. Teamwork is a very important part of all construction work and can help work to run smoothly and safeguard people's safety.

This unit has also explained the advantages and disadvantages of different types of communication. You will need to make sure that you always choose the most appropriate method of communication for the situation you are in. You also need to be confident in using all the different methods (letters, email, telephone, signs etc.) of communication.

You have seen some of the key moments when clear communication is vital for a team to work effectively. You will need to be able to demonstrate how key personnel should communicate to be effective.

The communicational skills that are explained within the unit are also vital in all tasks that you will undertake throughout your training and in life.

Good luck!

CHECK YOUR KNOWLEDGE

1 Which of these will need to be actioned after a breach of company rules?
- **a** a change to the work programme
- **b** disciplinary
- **c** a new procedure
- **d** mediation

2 Why are documents checked for conformity?
- **a** To meet the requirements of a contract.
- **b** To check employee's training.
- **c** To meet the requirements of CDM regulations.
- **d** To avoid problems, delays or confusion.

3 The purpose of a specification is:
- **a** to tell you how long a job will take
- **b** to tell you the quality of work, and sizes not shown on the drawing
- **c** to tell you the quantity of materials you will need
- **d** to tell you how much the job will cost

4 Why is an assembly drawing used?
- **a** To give all information needed to manufacture a component.
- **b** To show the basic sizes of a range of components.
- **c** To identify the structure of a proposed site.
- **d** To give a clear view of an elevation.

5 A written warning is a form of:
- **a** mediation
- **b** disciplinary
- **c** procedure
- **d** hierarchy

6 Day work rate means that you get paid:
- **a** a specific amount for every day you work
- **b** the same amount no matter what you do
- **c** every day, even if you don't work
- **d** weekly

7 What site paperwork is used to record hours worked?
- **a** day work sheet
- **b** job sheet
- **c** time sheet
- **d** variation order

8 To what scale are site plans usually drawn?
- **a** 1:500 or 1:200
- **b** 1:2500 or 1:1250
- **c** 1:100 or 1:50
- **d** 1:10 or 1:5

9 Which of these do not need to be communicated to the whole team?
- **a** alterations to drawings
- **b** variations to a contract
- **c** work restrictions
- **d** none of the above

10 What is the contract document that deals with repeated design information?
- **a** specification
- **b** schedule
- **c** plans and drawings
- **d** conditions of contract

UNIT 2003

Knowledge of building methods and construction technology 2

Whatever type of building is being constructed there are certain principles and elements that must be included. For example, both a block of flats and a warehouse have a roof, walls and a floor. These basic principles are applied across all the work carried out in construction and will apply to nearly all the projects you could work on. The primary areas this unit will look at are the principles behind walls, floors, roofs and internal work.

This unit supports NVQ Unit QCF 02 Conform to efficient work practices and QCF 03 Move and handle resources.

This unit also contains materials that support TAP Unit: Set out for masonry structures and contains material that supports the five generic units.

This unit will cover the following:

■ Principles behind walls, floors and roofs
■ Principles behind internal work
■ Storage and delivery of materials

K1. Principles behind walls, floors and roofs

All construction work requires working plans and drawings to complete the work. Drawings were covered earlier in Unit 2002 (pages 33–39).

It is important to realise that when buildings are designed at the planning stage the different types of materials, methods of construction and principles behind all components are discussed and the most suitable materials and methods are chosen.

Principles of construction

Before looking at the range of different structures it is important to understand some of the key principles of construction. These are insulation and structural stability.

Structural loading

The main parts of a building that are in place to carry a load are said to be in a constant state of **stress**.

There are three main types of stress – tension, compression and shear:

- **Tension** – pulls or stretches a material and can have a lengthening effect.
- **Compression** – squeezes the material and can have a shortening effect.
- **Shear** – occurs when one part of a component slips or slides over another causing a slicing effect.

To cause one of these types of stress a component or member must be under the strain of a load.

> **Remember**
>
> When drawings are completed the correct keys, symbols, abbreviations and hatchings are used so that the various components used in construction are easily recognised and can be constructed.

> **Key term**
>
> **Stress** – a constant force or system of forces exerted upon a body resulting in strain or deformation

Figure 3.1 The three types of stress

Compression   Tension   Shear

Within construction there are two main types of loading.

- **Dead load** – the weight of the building itself and the materials used to construct the building, including components such as floors and roofs.
- **Imposed loads** – any moveable loads such as furniture, as well as natural forces such as wind, rain and snow.

To cope with the loads that a building must withstand there are load-bearing structural members strategically placed throughout the building.

There are three main types of load-bearing members:

- **Horizontal members** – one of the most common types of horizontal member is a floor joist, which carries the load and transfers it back to its point of support. The horizontal member, when under loading, can bend and be in all three types of stress, with the top in compression, the bottom in tension and the ends in shear. The bending can be contained by using correctly stress-graded materials or by adding a load-bearing wall to support the floor.
- **Vertical members** – any walls or columns that are in place to transfer the loads from above (including from horizontal members) down to the substructure and foundations have vertical members. Vertical members are usually in a compression state.
- **Bracing members** – bracing members are usually fitted diagonally to form a triangle which stiffens the structure. Bracing members can be found in roofs and even on scaffolding. Bracing is usually in compression or tension.

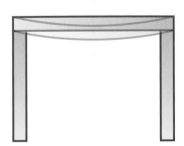

Figure 3.2 Horizontal structural members

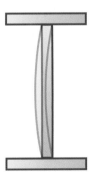

Figure 3.3 Vertical structural members

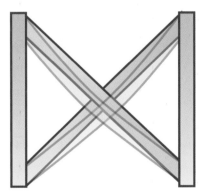

Figure 3.4 Bracing structural members

Damp proof course (DPC)

With sustainability and energy efficiency being talked about more and more the need to ensure that construction work is done with this in mind is vital. One of the main ways of ensuring that energy efficiency is maintained is by using correct insulation and a damp proof course.

A damp proof course (often shortened to DPC) or damp proof membrane (DPM) is a layer of non-absorbent material bedded on to a wall to prevent moisture penetrating into a building.

There are three main ways moisture can penetrate into a building:

- rising up from the ground
- through the walls
- moisture running downwards from the top of walls around openings or chimneys.

There are three types of DPC:

- flexible
- semi-rigid
- rigid.

Flexible DPC

Flexible DPC comes in rolls of various widths to suit requirements. Nowadays most rolls are made of pitch-polymer or polythene but bitumen can still be found. Metal can be used as a DPC (copper and lead) but because of the cost is mainly used in specialised areas. The most widely used and economic DPC material is polythene. Flexible DPC should always be laid upon a thin bed of mortar and lapped by a minimum of 100 mm on a corner or if joining a new roll.

Semi-rigid DPC

This type of DPC is normally made from blocks of asphalt melted and spread in coats to form a continuous membrane for tanking basements or underground work.

Rigid DPC

Rigid DPC uses solid material such as engineering bricks or slate, which were the traditional materials used. Slate is more expensive to use than other DPC materials and has no flexibility. If movement occurs the slate will crack, allowing damp to penetrate. Engineering bricks could be used for a garden wall if a DPC was required.

Tests on soil include:

- penetration tests – to establish density of soil
- compression tests – to establish shear strength of the soil or its bearing capacity
- various laboratory tests – to establish particle size, moisture content, humus content and chemical content.

Once all site investigations have been completed and all necessary information and data has been established in relation to the proposed building project, site clearance can take place.

Site clearance

The main purpose of site clearance is to remove existing buildings, waste, vegetation and, most importantly, the surface layer of soil referred to as topsoil. It is necessary to remove this layer of soil because it is unsuitable to build on. This surface layer of soil is difficult to compact down due to the high content of vegetable matter, which makes the soil soft and loose. The topsoil also contains various chemicals that encourage plant growth, which may adversely affect some structures over time.

The process of removing the topsoil can be very costly, in terms of both labour and transportation. The site investigations will determine the volume of topsoil that needs to be removed.

In some instances, the excavated topsoil may not be transported off site. Where building projects include garden plots, the topsoil may just need to be stored on site, thus reducing excessive labour and transportation costs. However, where this is the case, the topsoil must be stored well away from areas where buildings are to be erected or materials are to be stored, to prevent contamination of soils or materials.

Once the site clearance is complete, excavations for the foundations can start and the concrete foundations can be constructed.

Construction of concrete foundations

Trench excavation

In most modern-day construction projects, trenches are excavated by mechanical means. Although this is an expensive method, it reduces labour time and the risks associated with manual excavation work. Even with the use of machines to carry out excavations, an element of manual labour will still be needed to clean up the excavation work.

Find out

How are the different soil tests carried out?

How can plant growth affect some structures?

Did you know?

Site investigations or surveys will also establish the contours of the site. This will identify where certain areas of the site will need to be reduced or increased in height. An area of the site may need to be built up in order to mask surrounding features outside the boundaries of the proposed building project.

Figure 3.7 Removing soil from a site

Loose soil from both the base and sides of the trench will have to be removed, and the sides of the trench will have to be finished vertically.

Manual labour is still required for excavating trenches on some projects where machine access is limited and where only small strip foundations of minimum depths are required.

Trenches to be excavated are identified by lines attached to and stretched between profiles. This is the most accurate method of ensuring trenches are dug to the exact widths required.

Trench support

The type and extent of support required in an excavated trench will depend predominantly on the depth of the trench and the stability of the soil.

Traditionally, trench support was provided by using varying lengths and sizes of timber, which can easily be cut to required lengths. However, timber can become unreliable under certain loadings, pressures and weather conditions and can fail in its purpose.

More modern materials have been introduced as less costly and time-consuming methods of providing the required support. These materials include steel sheeting, rails and props. Trench support can be provided with a mixture of timber and steel components.

Concrete

Concrete is a mixture of cement, aggregates and water. The aggregate is normally in two parts:

- **fine aggregate** – sand and limestone dust
- **coarse aggregate** – gravel or limestone chippings.

The coarse aggregate is the bulk of the concrete, while the fine aggregate fills in the voids between the larger particles.

> **Did you know?**
>
> The Health and Safety Executive has produced detailed documents that deal exclusively with safety in excavations. These documents can be downloaded from the HSE website or obtained upon request direct from the HSE.
>
> Regulations relating to safety in excavations are set out in the Building Regulations and these must be strictly adhered to during the work.

> **Remember**
>
> All aggregates should be 'well graded' – they should range from small to large grains – so they fill in all the voids in the concrete.

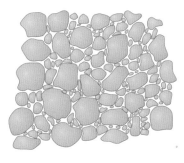

Well graded

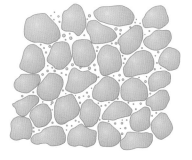

Poorly graded

Figure 3.8 Well-graded and poorly graded concrete

Windows

Windows are fitted to allow natural light to enter the building with minimal loss of heat. Again, windows come in a variety of shapes and styles. Glass that is fitted in a window can be decorative and heat-loss resistant.

Architraves and skirting

Architraves are decorative mouldings used to hide the gap between frames and the wall finish. Skirting is moulding that covers the gap between the floor and the base of a wall. These mouldings come in a variety of **profiles** such as torus and ogee.

Other mouldings can also be used, such as picture and dado rails.

Substance damage to building materials

There are a number of substances that can have a negative effect on building materials when they come into contact with them.

Water

Water can cause a range of problems for materials and can have a number of detrimental effects on them. Water can cause components to expand, which can add additional stress to joints and cause cracks or gaps to appear. Water can also cause some components to rust, reduce the effectiveness of insulation properties and damage interior finishes such as paint. Water in materials will increase the chances that they will be attacked by mould, fungi or insects.

Frost

Severe frost can cause water in exposed pipe-work to turn to ice. As it turns to ice, it expands and it is this expansion which can cause copper pipes to fracture or split. It is only when the ice thaws and becomes water again that the fracture becomes evident as the pipes or joints leak. Severe frost can also cause the moisture in wet brickwork to expand, forcing the front face of the brickwork to break away. This is known as spalling.

Chemicals

Chemicals can have a very detrimental effect on building materials. Most will cause some damage, and certain chemicals can corrode or even completely break down and destroy some materials.

Key term

Profile – the shape of a moulding when you cut through it

Find out

Use the Internet to research some common chemicals and the effects that they can have on a range of materials.

Safety tip

Chemicals can be dangerous – don't put yourself at risk and always follow instructions.

Heat and fire

Heat causes materials to expand, creating minor problems such as plastic doors not shutting correctly. It can also affect things such as paint finishes, the thermal properties of materials and the effectiveness of certain glues. Fire will destroy the majority of building materials if hot enough and left to burn. Steel's structural strength decreases dramatically under extreme heat.

Reducing the risk of damage

Materials can be treated to prevent or reduce the effects of these elements. The type of treatment used is usually chemical and care must be taken to ensure that the treatment will not cause other damage. Don't make matters worse when you are trying to improve them!

Products that provide protection to materials will come with manufacturers' instructions – be sure to follow these instructions.

Rectifying material deterioration

If any materials have deteriorated and need to be repaired or replaced then it is vital that the cause of deterioration is found and steps are taken to prevent reoccurrence.

This may mean treating the replacement materials or, in the case of water damage, repairing any leaks. The main methods used to protect and repair the main groups of materials are as follows:

- **Timber** can be protected by cutting out damaged parts. A protective coating, based on water, tar or solvents, can be placed on wood. These products are known as preservatives.
- **Metal materials** can be given protective coatings. Steel and iron can be coated in zinc, which will prevent rusting. This is known as galvanic protection.
- **Concrete and masonry** are protected by expansion joints, which provide a gap between adjoining slabs, allowing each slab space to expand. This helps prevent cracks.

K3. Storage and delivery of materials

Stock rotation and delivery times

When dealing with certain materials it is important to know about stock rotation, which ensures that the materials do not go past their use-by date. Materials such as plaster or cement have a use-by date on them; generally, such materials will set or go off around this date. Materials must be used before this happens.

Safety tip

All wood preservatives are toxic and should be handled with care.

92

When taking delivery of materials, place the newest items at the back. This will mean that the older materials are used first and will reduce the risk of them reaching their use-by date.

Delivery dates are also important: you want to ensure that materials are there when they need to be used, but you don't want them delivered weeks before they are needed as they will take up valuable storage space and can get damaged or expire.

The main types of materials affected by this are:

- cement
- plaster
- glue
- paints
- preservative coatings.

Checking deliveries to sites

When a delivery is made to a site, security will check that the delivery is due and that the materials are indeed for that site. The foreman or site agent will then look at the delivery note and check it against the order to ensure that what is being delivered is what was ordered.

The unloading of the materials can then take place, usually with a designated person checking the quality of the materials as well as checking the quantity against the delivery note. The materials should then be stored appropriately, as described above.

Tools used to transport materials

When handling materials it is important to know the safest way to carry things. Manual handling should be avoided if at all possible and mechanised equipment such as forklifts should be used instead.

If this is not possible or available, hand tools should be used. These include:

- wheelbarrows
- pallet trucks
- bag trolleys
- skips.

In some cases there is only one way that a material can be carried, for example mixed cement should only be moved in a wheelbarrow.

FAQ

How do I know if the materials I am using are strong enough to carry the load?

The specification will give you the details of the sizes and types of material that are to be used. You will need to refer to this document when you are selecting which materials to use.

Do I have to fix battens to a wall before I plasterboard it?

No. The method called dot and dab can be used where plaster is dabbed onto the back of the plasterboard and then pushed onto the wall.

Check it out

1 Describe the process that should happen before any construction work commences on a building project.
2 State three key factors that influence the design of a foundation and explain why.
3 Explain what is meant by the terms 'dead load' and 'imposed load'.
4 During a site investigation, certain data needs to be collected. Give a list of the key information that must be recorded during this investigation.
5 Why must excavation work be carefully planned before it is carried out?
6 Name three categories of soil.
7 Name three types of foundation. Complete sketches to show the key features of these types of foundation.
8 Explain how surface water can affect excavation work.
9 In a stepped foundation, what is the recommended maximum height of each concrete step?
10 State four of the main elements of building and explain briefly what each of them are.
11 List the three main types of stress.
12 Give a brief description of external walling.
13 What are the four main secondary elements? Why are they secondary?
14 Give a brief description of the process involved with lath and plaster.
15 What are the three main services?

Getting ready for assessment

The information contained in this unit, as well as continued practical assignments that you will carry out in your college or training centre, will help you with preparing for both your end-of-unit test and the diploma multiple-choice test. It will also aid you in preparing for the work that is required for the synoptic practical assignments.

The information in this unit will build on the information that you may have acquired during Level 1 CC1003 and will help you understand the basics of your own trade as well as the basic information on several other trade areas.

You will need to be familiar with:

- the principles behind foundations, walls, floors and roofs
- the principles behind internal work
- storage and delivery of building materials.

It is important to understand what other trades do in relation to you and how the work they do affects you and your work. It is also good to know how the different components of a building are constructed and how these tie in with the tasks that you carry out. You must always remember that there are a number of tasks being carried out on a building site at all times, and many of these will not be connected to the work you are carrying out. It is useful to remember the communication skills you learned in Unit 2002, as these will be important for working with other trades on site. You will also need to be familiar with specifications and contract documents, to know the type of construction work other crafts will be doing around you on site.

For learning outcome one you saw the range of different structures, and how they maintain structural stability and quality of insulation. It is important that structures have precise working drawings to complete their construction accurately. You will need to be able to sketch a section through building elements and components.

This unit has explained the different construction methods for foundations, walls, floors and roofs. Although you will not be working on all these elements, you need to be familiar with the work undertaken on them in order to plan when to carry out your own work. You will need to be able to complete a programme of work for a simple two-storey construction. To do this you will need to understand the jobs that other trades will need to carry out on these parts of the building.

Remember, that a sound knowledge of construction methods and materials will be very useful during your training as well as later in your professional career.

Good luck!

CHECK YOUR KNOWLEDGE

1 What is the most popular and widely used insulation?
a polystyrene sheets
b rigid foam
c glass mineral wool
d rock wool

2 The purpose of any foundation of a building is to ensure that all dead and imposed loads are safely absorbed and transmitted through to the natural foundation. What is meant by a 'dead load'?
a the weight of the structure
b the weight that may be imposed on the structure itself
c the combined weight of the structure and other loads imposed upon it
d the weight of the concrete foundation imposed on the natural subsoil or natural foundation

3 The final decision for the suitability and in particular the depth of the foundation and thickness of concrete will rest with whom?
a structural design team
b architect
c local authority
d client

4 The type of foundation used for a small domestic dwelling or low rise structure is:
a wide strip foundation
b short bored piled foundation
c pad foundation
d narrow strip foundation

5 Where a stepped foundation is used, the height of each step should not be greater than the thickness of the concrete and not greater than:
a 250 mm
b 300 mm
c 450 mm
d 600 mm

6 In a stepped foundation, the overlap of the concrete to that below should not be less than:
a 250 mm
b 300 mm
c 450 mm
d 600 mm

7 Which of the following are primary elements?
a roofs
b windows
c foundations
d all of the above

8 Flat roofs are constructed in a similar way to:
a suspended timber floors.
b floating floors
c truss roofing
d cut roofing

9 Which of the following secondary elements provides access between rooms?
a skirting
b doors
c windows
d linings

10 Which of the following are finishing elements?
a plaster
b glazing
c dado rail
d all of the above

Know how to prepare surfaces for decoration 2

Surface preparation is very important for producing a high-quality finish. In this unit we will look at some typical surfaces you may find yourself working on during your career, along with appropriate preparation tasks for each surface.

It is important that all surface contaminants such as dirt, oil, rust and loose or flaking existing coatings are removed. If these contaminants are not removed, it could affect whether the paint or paper will adhere (stick) to the surface.

This unit also contains material that supports NVQ unit QCF 332 Prepare surfaces for Painting/Decorating.

This unit also contains material that supports TAP Unit Prepare surfaces for Painting/Decorating.

This unit covers the following learning outcomes:

- Preparing timbers and timber sheet products ready to receive finishing systems
- Preparing metal surfaces ready to receive finishing systems
- Preparing trowelled finishes and plasterboard ready to receive finishing systems
- Removing previously applied paint and paper ready to receive finishing systems
- Rectifying surface conditions
- Repairing and making good surfaces

Unit 2019 Know how to prepare surfaces for decoration 2

K1. Preparing timbers and timber sheet products ready to receive finishing systems

Timber is one of the most commonly used materials in construction. You will encounter timber in a wide range of situations, both internal and external.

Applications of timber and timber sheet products

Types of timber

Timber is classified as either softwood or hardwood. This can sometimes be confusing as not all hardwoods are physically hard or softwoods soft. Hardwood and softwood refers to the **botanical** differences and not the strength of the timber. Hardwood trees are **deciduous**, broad leaved, with an encased seed. Softwood trees are usually **evergreen** with needles and seeds held in cones.

Key terms

Botanical – the classification of trees based on scientific study

Deciduous – the name given to a type of tree that sheds it leaves every year

Evergreen – the name given to a type of tree that keeps its leaves all year around

Name	Appearance	Properties/Description	Uses
Redwood (commonly known as pine)		Moderately strong for its weight with average durability. Quality of finish depends on knots and amount of resin. Capable of smooth, clean finish and can be glued, stained, varnished and painted.	Used for interior or exterior work and for carcassing and finish joinery
Whitewood (also known as European Spruce)		Similar to redwood in strength and durability. Takes glue, nails and screws well and can produce a good finish.	Similar uses to redwood
Western red cedar		Not as strong as redwood but has naturally occurring oils which prevent insect attack. Doesn't need treating as will stand up to severe weather and turns a silvery colour when exposed.	Externally for good-quality timber buildings, saunas, etc.

Table 19.1 Commonly used softwoods

Friable surfaces

A friable surface crumbles away easily when you rub your hand over it. Examples of this kind of surface include weathered cement rendering or old, spalled brickwork. Paint applied to these surfaces will also crumble off. A stabilising solution can be applied. Brush the surface down with a stiff brush to remove loose particles. Then apply the solution, which soaks deep into the surface acting like a glue, binding it down.

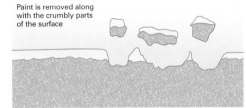

Figure 19.29 Paint applied to a friable surface

Rectification processes and defects

Many of the common rectification processes are covered elsewhere in this book including scraping (page 119), abrading (page 103), brushing (page 113), washing down for a finish (page 128) and face putty (below).

Chalking and powdering

This is a fine powder created on a coating by weathering. Heavy chalking leads to film erosion and is caused by low grade, highly pigmented paints or by using interior paints on exterior surfaces. Remove chalk by scrubbing with a stiff bristle brush, or using a power washer, and then rinse the area.

Wrinkling or shrivelling

This is a rough, crinkled paint surface caused by contaminated surfaces, previous coatings that have not dried correctly, hot conditions or exposure to rain, dew, fog or high humidity before drying. To rectify, scrape or sand the substrate then recoat the surface, making sure conditions are correct and each coat dries fully.

Defective putty

When removing old paint from window frames, some of the putty is likely to break away. After surface preparations have been completed, the bare timber can be primed and any defective putty replaced with linseed oil putty.

Any old putty that has not broken away will be firmly adhered to the window frame and will not need to be replaced. However any gaps between the old putty and the glass must be completely sealed by forcing in linseed oil putty using a putty knife.

Safety tip

If you are working on a bonded asbestos surface, make sure you take precautions and wear the correct PPE, for example, gloves and a face mask.

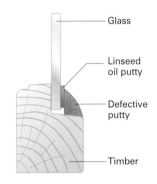

Figure 19.30 Defective putty

Other surface conditions

Surface condition	Appearance	Description/Cause
Cissing		Coatings applied on contaminated surfaces, which prevent adhesion. Allow paint to dry before using wet and dry abrasive paper to abrade the surface. Wash down with warm water and detergent then rinse.
Bittiness		Small particles of dirt on a wet coating. Abrade the surface then dust down and remove dirt before repainting.
Runs, sags and curtains		Too much coating applied to a surface and paint running down. Do not overload brush and spread out coating.

Table 19.21 Surface defects and causes

Did you know?

When washing a surface, you should always start at the bottom and work upwards. This avoids streaking of painted surfaces, which can damage the finish.

Cleaning surfaces

When washing down a surface, it is very important that the correct washing agent is used. Dirt can be removed with sugar soap or a mild detergent. Oily and greasy marks will probably only come off with the use of white spirit or turps applied with a cloth or brush. Wax polish will need to be washed off with a suitable solvent or warm water and sugar soap. You may also find that smoke needs to be removed from surfaces. Make sure that the area is thoroughly rinsed after cleaning and allowed to dry completely.

When cleaning a surface you will need to know what the surface coating is. Wipe the surface using a clean rag with a stain remover. If the rag is still clean, the surface is solvent based. If it is dirty, the surface is water based.

K6. Repairing and making good surfaces

This unit has discussed how the different types of surfaces – timber, brickwork, blockwork, plaster, cement and plasterboard – can be affected by defects, and the methods of correcting these defects.

It is pointless to prepare and paint a surface if it is damp or if weather conditions are wet or very cold as this will affect the paint finish or its ability to dry. These are environmental considerations and must be taken into account during surface preparation.

Wet, unseasoned timber or wet, newly plastered or washed walls must be given an adequate drying out period. Applying any surface coating before drying could lead to blistering, peeling, discoloration and staining.

Decorating in cold conditions (below 5°C) or wet weather can result in:

- failure of water-based paints to dry (due to lack of adhesion)
- washing off of water-based paints
- blooming of alkyd finishes (for example, loss of gloss and a cloudy surface)
- rain pitting of alkyd finishes
- peeling.

FAQ

Can I use caulk to fill holes in surfaces?

No! It is not advisable to use caulk to fill holes and cracks because you cannot abrade caulk when it dries. This is because its flexible properties do not let it harden off. Caulk is only recommended for filling the tops of skirting board and around architrave to seal any gaps.

How long do you leave a steam stripper on a surface when removing wall coverings?

It depends on how many layers of wallpaper are on the surface. However, you should not allow the steam stripper to stay in any one place too long as you can cause the plaster on the surface to 'blow'. This is when the plaster lifts off the surface therefore creating a much bigger defect that needs repairing.

Why do you have to 'wet in' prior to applying fillers to holes and cracks?

You 'wet in' before applying fillers to holes and cracks to help with the adhesion of the filler and to remove any excess dust and debris that has not been fully removed during the preparation stage.

When removing rust and millscale from metal, is it not better to make sure that you totally remove all traces and make the surface clean and shiny?

Although the rust has to be removed from the metal, it is not advisable to make sure that the surface is clean and shiny as, when you try to apply the paint system, the primer will not be able to adhere to the surface as there will be no key for the paint to stick to.

Check it out

1   Prepare a report explaining the differences between softwoods and hardwoods and explaining where you may encounter them when working. You should make reference to the properties and possible defects that each type of wood may have.

2   Prepare a method statement, with diagrams, explaining how to use abrasives for timber surfaces.

3   Explain, with diagrams, each stage that may occur during corrosion, focusing on the process of electrolysis. Explain the advantages and disadvantages this process may have.

4   Complete a method statement explaining the best methods for removing rust from metal surfaces. Your statement should explain how to prepare these surfaces for the application of a primer.

5   When spot priming metal surfaces, name two different primers used and which metals they would be applied to. Explain why these primers would be used.

6   Describe the different types of trowelled and plasterboard finishes you may encounter when working and explain some of the qualities of each.

7   Explain how defective rendering may occur and what can be done to rectify this.

8   Using diagrams and photographs, collect examples of the main paint and paper defects you may encounter while working. Explain how these arise and what can be done to rectify them.

9   Prepare a method statement explaining how to remove paint with heat, including reference to the health and safety practices that must be followed to ensure safe working.

10 Explain the purpose behind cleaning surfaces before work and state the best tools and equipment to use for these.

11 Explain the potential problems that can arise when plaster is affected by heat and moisture.

Getting ready for assessment

The information contained in this unit, as well as continued practical assignments that you will carry out in your college or training centre, will help you in preparing for both your end-of-unit test and the diploma multiple-choice test. It will also aid you in preparing for the work that is required for the synoptic practical assignments.

When painting and decorating you will need to be able to prepare a range of surfaces to receive coatings. This will include not only new surfaces made from a range of materials, but also surfaces that have previously been painted or decorated. To carry this out you will need to know the techniques and methods used to prepare these surfaces, as well as repairing and making good any defects or damage to the surface before work.

You will need to be familiar with:

- preparing timbers and timber sheet products ready to receive finishing systems
- preparing metal surfaces ready to receive finishing systems
- preparing trowelled finishes and plasterboard to receive finishing systems
- removing previously applied paint and paper ready to receive finishing systems
- rectifying surface conditions
- repairing and making good surfaces

Most of these learning outcomes revolve around learning about the implications of working with different surfaces, and dealing with the defects that could occur as you work with them. For example, for learning outcome three you will need to select the correct processes for rectifying the defects you have learned about when working with plaster, plasterboards, brickwork and blockwork. You will also need to select the correct preparation processes for these surfaces, using the correct tools, equipment and materials to ensure a high-quality finish. Using all of this you will need to prepare the surface to receive the finish, ensuring that you are working safely and being environmentally aware.

The knowledge you have gained about the different types of surfaces, and the preparation techniques needed for each, will prepare you for any aspect of the practical test where you will need to prepare or repair or surface. These same skills will be vital throughout your career as a painter and decorator.

Before you carry out any work, you should set out a plan of action, which will tell you the order in which you need to do things. It will also record a rough timescale for the work you need to carry out, in order to make sure that you complete everything you need to do safely. You will need to refer back to this plan at each stage to make sure that you are not making any mistakes as you work, or missing out any part of the process that you need to work through. Without checking this you could make some serious mistakes that could have an impact on the final build.

Your speed in carrying out any tasks in a practice setting will also help to prepare you for the time set for the test. However, you must never rush the test! Always make sure you are working safely. Make sure throughout the test that you are wearing the appropriate PPE and using tools correctly.

Good luck!

CHECK YOUR KNOWLEDGE

1 Which of the following is not a classification of wood?:
   a hardwood
   b softwood
   c gypsum
   d timber sheet product

2 Why is knotting applied to softwood structures?
   a to prime knots in them
   b to undercoat knots in them
   c to seal knots in them
   d none of the above

3 When using fillers what should be done before use?
   a area should be dusted
   b area should be wetted in prior to applying filler
   c area should have loose materials removed
   d all of the above

4 What is the best material to use to fill gaps around the tops of skirting boards and around frames?
   a caulk
   b stopper
   c filler
   d all of the above

5 When washing wall surfaces prior to decoration where is the best position to start?
   a the top
   b the bottom
   c the sides
   d anywhere on the wall

6 Which grade of abrasive paper would you class as coarse?
   a P20
   b P80
   c P220
   d P320

7 Which primer is used on galvanised metals?
   a universal primer
   b mordant solution
   c metal primer
   d zinc phosphate primer

8 Which of these describe dry lining?
   a plasterboards fixed to stud walling
   b plasterboards fixed to solid walls
   c plasterboards not used
   d none of the above

9 After using paint stripper on a surface how do you decontaminate the area?
   a wipe down with a cloth
   b dry it off
   c wash it down
   d sand it off

10 When removing vinyl wallpapers from surfaces it is best to what?
   a score the paper first
   b wet the paper first
   c peel the vinyl first
   d all of the above

Know how to apply paint systems by brush and roller 2

Paint can be applied to a surface in a variety of different ways. Each method of application has its own advantages and disadvantages and should be chosen according to the type of surface, the type of paint and the finished effect that is desired. Applying the surface coating can be one of the cheapest, quickest, easiest and most effective tasks a decorator can perform.

The most common methods used are brush and roller, and you will need to know the best method to use for the main types of coating you will encounter during your career.

This unit contains material that supports NVQ unit QCF 333 Apply paint systems by brush and roller.

This unit also contains material that supports TAP Unit Apply paint systems by brush and roller.

This unit will cover the following learning outcomes:

- Preparing the work area and protecting surrounding areas, furniture and fittings
- Preparing materials for application, and applying water-based and solvent-based coatings by brush and roller
- Cleaning, maintaining and storing brushes and rollers
- Storing materials

K1. Preparing the work area and protecting surrounding areas, furniture and fittings

Before any decorating is started, the most important task for the decorator is to protect any areas, items, fixtures and fittings that are not being worked on which could be damaged.

It is very important that, before you start any work, you look around and make sure that all items are protected by removing them or covering them with the appropriate material. Damage caused during decorating could be very costly, both to the decorator's pocket and reputation.

You will be familiar with the work needed to prepare and protect surfaces from Level 1. This section will remind you of the principles when protecting surfaces.

Considerations for preparing the working area

When preparing internal or external work areas before carrying out the application of paint systems you first need to make sure that all dust and debris (flakes of paint, bristles, pieces of abrasive paper and so on) have been removed. This ensures that no contamination can occur to the surfaces while coatings are still wet.

Domestic properties

The following areas will need to be protected when you are working in domestic properties.

- **Doors** – easiest to remove and store in a container in a safe and dry place. If not, cover the door with masking paper or sheet.
- **Windows** – always remove curtains, storing them neatly in a plastic bag. Remove the pelmet from the curtain pole and cover it with a protective sheet or store in a safe dry place. Curtain poles and tracks are best removed from the work area. Blinds should be retracted and removed from their brackets.
- **Wall-mounted fixtures and fittings** – shelving is easy to remove and store. Glass shelving should be wrapped in newspaper or bubble wrap. Light fittings should be removed by a qualified electrician, although a light can be turned off at the mains. The fuse must be removed from the mains fuse box with a warning notice put in place to prevent the power from being reconnected.

- **Room furniture** – this should be removed from the room or, if this is not possible, it should be placed in the centre of the room and covered.
- **Carpets and floors** – the client should arrange removal of floor coverings. If not removed, dust sheets, polythene sheeting and masking tape should be used to protect them.

Commercial properties

The following areas will need to be protected when you are working in commercial properties.

- **Workstation** – this refers to items of furniture in a commercial property, such as work desks and chairs, computer stations, filing cabinets and telephones, etc. These items should be removed if possible or should be protected by dust sheets and plastic sheeting, depending on the job being completed.
- **Lighting** – this should be protected by clear polythene sheeting and masking tape to prevent any damage while applying coatings by brush, roller or spray.
- **Machinery** – the weight of most machinery means that it is advisable to protect it by using dust sheets, plastic sheeting and tarpaulin.
- **Equipment** – remove any items of equipment if possible and protect in the same way as machinery if the items cannot be removed to a safer area.

Types of masking tape and applying and removing tape

Masking paper and tape is widely used to help protect surfaces. Masking paper can be self-adhesive but is otherwise held in place by tape. Low-tack masking tape is often used as it is easy to remove. The types of masking tape are shown below.

Masking tape	Description
Exterior masking	Heavy duty, waterproof, strong and UV resistant. Adheres well to surfaces. Used to fix protective sheeting to frames when tenting.
Interior masking	Low tack, ideal for protecting fixtures and fittings. Can keep dust sheets in place. Will not pull coating off surfaces when removed.
Crepe masking	Tan coloured, made from solvent and moisture-resistant material. Can be stretched allowing it to mask irregular surfaces.
7-day masking	Can be left in place for up to seven days without damaging surfaces. Used on more demanding surfaces (for example, glazes).

Table 20.1 Types of masking tape

Appropriate uses for dust sheets, tarpaulin and corrugated sheeting

Sheet materials such as dust sheets, tarpaulin and corrugated sheeting are the most commonly used and useful of protective materials. Sheeting can protect against paint and paste splashes and spillages and also small particles that are created when sanding or scraping.

Remember

To prolong the life and use of dust sheets you should always make sure that they are looked after. Always shake thoroughly after use to remove any debris, then fold them up correctly so they are neat and tidy. Store in a dry area and, if possible, on a shelving unit to help them keep their shape and stay clean.

Type of protective material	Description	Factors affecting use
Cotton twill dust sheets	Best-quality dust sheets Double fold to increase thickness Protect flooring and furniture Available in different weights and sizes	Not easily disturbed Expensive to purchase and clean Heavy paint spillage can soak through Absorbs chemicals and can be a fire risk
Polythene dust sheets	Similar in use to cotton twill dust sheets Waterproof Less professional looking than cotton twill	Cheap Heavy paint spills don't soak through and don't absorb chemicals Do not remain in place well
Tarpaulin	Made from different materials (rubber-coated cotton, heavy cotton canvas, PVC-coated nylon, nylon scrim) Used on and around scaffolding Used when washing down surfaces or steam stripping	Mostly 6 m by 4 m. Larger sizes can be ordered. Protective against moisture and bad weather conditions
Corrugated sheeting	Purchased in sheet form and laid over the floor	More expensive but better protection against more 'aggressive' work

Table 20.2 Types of protective sheeting

K2. Preparing materials for application, and applying water-based and solvent-based coatings by brush and roller

Characteristics and function of component parts of brushes and rollers

Paintbrushes and rollers remain the most common methods for applying paint to a surface. You will need to be familiar with the components of each of these. You should be familiar with the types of brushes and rollers, as well as their components, from Level 1.

Find out

What are the differences between the two types of roller frame (cage and stick)?

	Description	Components
Brushes	• Bristles (filling) made from pure bristle, synthetic fibres, natural fibres or a combination • Must be thoroughly cleaned after use • Always store brushes flat and never upright on the filling because this will permanently change the shape of the filling and make the brush useless	• Ferrule – metal part of the brush, usually made from copper or nickel-plated steel • Fixed to the stock either by riveting to the handle or seamed to the joint • Setting – fixing or gluing of bristles in place
Rollers	• Used to coat large surfaces • Specially shaped rollers are available • Must be thoroughly cleaned after use • Extension poles are attached to give additional reach	• Sleeve – holds the paint. Type of sleeve depends on coating to be applied • Frame – cage or stick type

Table 20.3 Types of brushes and rollers

Types of surface coatings

Surface coatings are applied in order to do the following:

- **Protect** – steel can be prevented from corroding due to rust and wood can be prevented from rotting due to moisture and insect attack
- **Decorate** – the appearance of a surface can be improved or given a special effect (for example, marbling, wood graining)
- **Sanitise** – a surface can be made more hygienic with the application of a surface coating, preventing penetration and accumulation of germs and dirt. Also allows easier cleaning.

Figure 20.1 Flat brushes

Figure 20.2 Roller sleeves

Figure 20.3 Roller frame (single arm cage type)

Key term

Sanitise – to make something clean and free of germs

- **Identify** – different colours or types of surface coating can be used to distinguish areas or components (for example, pipework identified using the British Standards Institution's colour coding system).

Paint

Paint is either water based or solvent based. Water-based paint means that the main liquid part of the paint is water. Solvent-based paint means that a chemical has been used instead of water to dissolve the other components of the paint. When paint is applied to a surface, the water or the solvent evaporates into the air leaving the other components behind on the surface.

Water-based paint provides a moisture screen to prevent water from penetrating the surface. Solvent-based paint also forms a waterproof layer, preventing the formation of rot. Solvent-based paints are better for use with timber as they have a greater adhesion.

Paint should have the correct consistency – this refers to how thin or thick it is. Paints such as non-drip gloss are classed as thick paints and are known as thixotropic paint. Thixotropic agents give paint gel-like properties. Once in place the paint will turn back into a gel, reducing the chances of runs or drips.

Paint should be flexible, too, as certain surfaces have a small amount of movement. Paint also needs to stretch and shrink in response to atmospheric conditions such as humidity (this is called elasticity).

Opacity and adhesion are also important properties of a coating or paint. Opacity refers to the covering power of the paint. If the opacity is not correct, the coating or paint will be too transparent and will not block out the surface it is being applied to. If a coating or paint does not have the correct adhesion ('stickability') it will not stick to the surface.

Some types of paint contain chemicals known as isocyanate groups. These chemicals give off vapours (gases), which irritate the airways (windpipe and lungs) in people who inhale them and could cause conditions such as asthma.

Components of paint

All paints are made up with different components, each of which has its own purpose in the make up of the paint.

Safety tip

Solvents used in solvent-based paints are usually toxic and highly flammable so take proper precautions when using them. Water-based products were developed as a safer alternative to solvent-based paints. Always check any safety information with paints, avoid contact with skin or eyes and use correct PPE.

Pigment

The pigment is the solid component of the paint. This is the substance that makes up the colour of a coating. It also helps the film former protect the substrate. Pigments are classified as either organic or inorganic.

- **organic** – means that the material is natural, such as peat earth and oil

- **inorganic** – means that the pigment has come from coloured earth and is ground down to a fine powder such as raw umber and yellow ochre. These are also made from metals which have been chemically treated to turn them into fine powders such as white lead and iron oxide and also from chemicals which have been heat treated into zinc chromate.

Film former

The film former is also known as the medium or binder. It converts the liquid coating to a solid dry film. It also binds the pigment particles together, provides a gloss to the coating and helps the coating adhere to the surface. It provides resistance to water, chemicals and abrasion and gives elasticity to the film. It is a **resin** and determines the performance of the paint (how long it lasts) and the degree of gloss (shine).

The most commonly used film formers are drying oils (such as linseed oil, soya bean oil, tung oil or dehydrated castor oil) and resins, for example copal, alkyd, epoxy, polyurethane, rubber, lac and PVA (polyvinyl acetate).

> **Key term**
>
> **Resin** – this can be either natural (produced by plants and trees) or man-made (plastic)

Extender

Extenders allow certain coatings to be applied with ease and give greater adhesive properties to undercoats. They are obtained from natural materials, which are ground to a fine powder. This powder is usually white and therefore does not have any influence on the colour of the coating. These extenders are usually known as 'mineral whites'.

Extenders also give bulk to certain coatings which do not contain sufficient pigment content and aid film thicknes, which is why they are also known as fillers. They provide added hardness to coating films making them more durable.

> **Did you know?**
>
> Water-based resins are referred to as latex, as in latex coatings, and are made from natural or synthetic resins mixed with oils such as coumarone resin/tung oil or alkyd resin/linseed oil.

Dilutents

Dilutents are colourless and transparent and are used in all coatings. They are also known as solvents or thinners. They form part of the liquid state of the coating and evaporate during drying. When wet they allow fast application and help primers penetrate absorbent surfaces.

Dilutent	Description
Water	Readily available, cheap to purchase, used as a thinner for all emulsion paints
Alcohols and Ketones	Chemically produced, used in methylated spirits and as a thinner for spirit paint and varnishes
Hydrocarbons	Obtained from distillation of crude oil, used in white spirits and chlorinated paints
Ethers	Chemically produced, used as solvents for cellulose resins
Esters	Derivatives of acids, include different acetates such as ethyl and methyl acetated. Used as solvents for nitro-cellulose finishes
Chlorinated hydrocarbons	Produced by mixing chlorine with methane (very toxic). Used in paint removers and as a degreasing agent

Table 20.4 Types of dilutent

Driers

Driers are additives (water for emulsions and thinners for oil-based coatings) incorporated by the manufacturer into the drying oil. Extra driers are added to coatings to speed up the drying process. This is done by helping the film former absorb oxygen. Overuse of driers can cause cracking and shrivelling.

Some additives, such as anti-frothing agents and biocides, are found in emulsion paints and are added to give the emulsion more properties to prevent the coat freezing or foaming and to control mould growth and pigment stability.

Components of emulsion paints

Emulsion paints also contain substances such as fillers (extenders), catalysts, stabilisers, adhesion enhancers, emulsifiers and texturisers. These produce different results, such as thickening the film or increasing the volume of the coating.

Find out

Use the Internet and other resources to find out more about the components used to create emulsion paints.

Alkyd gloss

Alkyd gloss paint is solvent based and is usually used over a solvent-based alkyd undercoat. It is often used to protect joinery.

The advantages of alkyd gloss paint are that it:

- has good covering power (with the exception of strong yellows, reds and oranges)
- provides a good waterproof barrier
- provides a durable, easy-clean, high-gloss finish
- is available in a wide range of colours.

The disadvantages of alkyd gloss paint include:

- white alkyd gloss is prone to yellowing, or chalking, and loses its gloss on exteriors after a number of years
- it becomes brittle with age, which means that it is prone to cracking and flaking when it cannot accommodate any movement in the timber surface
- the waterproof nature of the finish prevents any water trapped within the surface from escaping, which can lead to blistering of the paint system or even wet rot.

Water-based gloss

Water-based gloss is made from acrylic polymers and is permeable, small holes in the coating allow air to reach the surface. Advantages of water-based gloss paint are that it:

- is easier to apply than alkyd gloss
- provides a flexible, non-yellowing film
- does not give off toxic fumes when drying
- means equipment can be easily washed out in water after use
- dries quickly in dry, warm conditions
- is resistant to alkalis
- does not chalk upon ageing.

Disadvantages of water-based gloss paint are that it:

- does not provide a high-gloss finish
- does not provide a seal between the glass and putties on timber window frames
- it can freeze, both on the surface and in the tin, due to its water content, and drying can be retarded by cold, damp conditions
- can be washed off exterior surfaces by rain while still wet
- is not as resistant to abrasion as alkyd gloss.

Undercoats

Undercoats, or intermediate coats as they are sometimes called, are designed to provide a sound base for the finish coats by providing:

- opacity (the ability to cover and hide the underlying coating)
- adequate film build for protection and finish quality.

Ordinary oil-based undercoats can become brittle with age, reducing the performance of the finishing paint system. Water-based undercoats do not perform well under solvent-based paints, particularly on exteriors.

For further information on undercoats, see Table 20.5 on pages 143–44.

Finishes

A finish is the top layer of paint – the one that will be seen. Matt and silk emulsions are the most commonly used type of finish on interior wall and ceiling surfaces. Matt emulsion is smooth, non-reflective (not glossy), quick-drying and available in countless colours. Silk emulsion is washable and gives a sheen finish when dry. It is ideal for areas such as kitchens and bathrooms. Vinyl soft sheen is a modern subtle alternative to vinyl matt and silk emulsions, drying to a soft mid-sheen and suitable for most wall and ceiling surfaces.

For more information on matt and silk vinyl emulsion finishes, see Table 20.5 on pages 143–44.

Eggshell finishes are durable paints suitable for interior use, particularly areas of high-humidity such as in kitchens and bathrooms. Unstirred, the paint has a semi-gel consistency that doesn't drip from the brush but liquefies on application. Alternatively, the paint can be beaten to a full-bodied fluid consistency, recommended for roller or spray application.

Varnish

Varnish is a transparent finish applied to wood. It comes in matt, satin and gloss varieties and provides a tough water- and heat-resistant protective coating. The components of varnish are as follows:

- **drying oil** – this is a substance such as linseed oil, tung oil or walnut oil, which dries to form a hardened solid film

> **Did you know?**
>
> Water-based eggshell paints are becoming more popular than oil-based eggshell paints because they do not give off strong fumes

However, new regulations were introduced in 2010 requiring lower VOC levels in all materials produced in the UK. This includes solvent- and water-based coatings, thinners and cleaning agents.

The British Coatings Industry has adopted a VOC labelling scheme to inform users about the levels of organic solvents and other volatile materials present. All companies are now required to add the VOC information to their product to warn about the pollution that the product contributes to the atmosphere.

There are five bands of VOCs.

Minimal	VOC content 0% to 0.29%, for example, acrylic primer/undercoat and masonry paints
Low	VOC content 0.3% to 7.99%, for example, water-based coatings (matt/silk emulsions, acrylic eggshells)
Medium	VOC content 8% to 24.99%, for example, acrylic glosses
High	VOC content 25% to 50%, for example, non-drip gloss, one-coat gloss, solvent-based eggshell, satinwood, wood primer, alkali-resisting primer, all purpose primer, heavy duty floor paints
Very high	VOC content more than 50%, for example, stabilising primers

Table 20.9 VOC bands

Each coating is assigned a particular letter which again should be identified on all labelling:

a – matt coatings for interior walls and ceilings

b – glossy coatings for interior walls and ceilings

c – coatings for exterior walls of mineral substrates

d – interior/exterior trim and cladding paints for wood, metal and plastic

e – interior/exterior trim varnishes and woodstains

f – minimal build wood stains

g – primers

h – binding primers

i – one-pack performance coatings

j – two-pack performance coatings

k – multi-coloured coatings

l – decorative effect coatings.

Did you know?

Some products and materials that a decorator will use are exempt in the new legislation as this only refers to coatings. The most common products are colourings for tinting, sugar soaps, brush cleaners, fillers and sealants/caulks.

Key term

Cutting in – the action of applying paint to one surface while keeping paint off an adjoining surface. Apply the paint in sections small enough to handle and in a vertical (up and down) motion, then cross the paint in a sideways motion with the brush in order to spread it evenly

Figure 20.7 Cutting in

Did you know?

Multiple wall areas can be painted if you are working with another painter as each painter would have a specific task. This method of working will speed up the whole process and enable the job to be completed ahead of time.

Remember

Using a roller and extension pole will make it a lot easier to apply the coating to a ceiling, but you can use a brush.

Sequence of painting room areas and components

Before starting to paint there are some key factors to consider:

- **preparation** – no surface should be painted unless it is sound, firm, clean and dry
- **environment** – make sure you are painting in conditions that will allow drying to take place
- **film thickness** – the paint must be of an adequate thickness. This is usually achieved by applying three coats of solvent-based (one coat each of primer, undercoat and gloss) or two coats of emulsion and acrylic water-based paints.

Room areas

This section will look at the methods used to paint each of the main areas you will deal with when painting. For the painting of a room it is best to follow this order:

- ceiling
- wall areas
- woodwork (doors, skirting boards, etc).

Ceilings

The first stage in painting a ceiling is to '**cut in**' the ceiling.

- Use the edge of the brush to create a clean line between wall and ceiling to avoid any paint marks appearing on the walls.
- Cut-in around the light fitting.
- Apply the coating using a roller and an extension pole.
- Paint should be applied in smooth, parallel actions. Overlap each application by a third to keep a wet edge and hide any joining lines.
- Once dry repeat with a second coating.

Broad walls

Usually an emulsion is used for walls, but sometimes solvent or oil-based paints such as eggshell can be used.

- 'Cut in' the top of the wall to the ceiling and any windows or doors and skirting board (linear work).
- Use the edge of the brush to get nice straight lines then turn the brush on its side and paint a band of about 8–9 cm. This will allow you to apply the remaining paint with a roller and avoid touching the ceiling or woodwork.
- Each wall area should be painted separately.

Getting ready for assessment

The information contained in this unit, as well as continued practical assignments that you will carry out in your college or training centre, will help you in preparing for both your end-of-unit test and the diploma multiple-choice test. It will also aid you in preparing for the work that is required for the synoptic practical assignments.

To complete any work as a painter or decorator you will need to know how to prepare a working area, protecting any property belonging to the client that may be nearby. For applying paint systems you will need to be confident with applying a range of surface coverings, both water-based and solvent-based with brushes and rollers. As with all practical work you will need to protect and store equipment correctly, as this will ensure that the equipment has a longer lifetime.

You will need to be familiar with:

- preparing the work area and protecting surrounding areas, furniture and fittings
- preparing materials for application and applying water-based and solvent-based coatings by brush and roller
- cleaning, maintaining and storing brushes and rollers
- storing materials

For learning outcome two you will need to be able to select the correct application tools and equipment for a wide range of surface coatings. To do this you will need to apply the knowledge you have gained about the different requirements of the surfaces you may encounter and the qualities of the available surface coatings. You will need to be able to select the surface coating that will work best for the surface you are covering. You will also need to be able to finish the job properly, allowing correct drying times and avoiding the creation of any defects in the paintwork. To give a job the best possible final appearance, you will also need to know about the qualities of different colours, in order to select the best shade and hue to match both the room and the lighting conditions it will be seen under.

Before you carry out any work, think of a plan of action, which will tell you the order you need to do things in. It will also record a rough timescale for the work you need to carry out, in order to make sure that you complete everything you need to do safely. You will need to refer back to this plan at each stage to make sure that you are not making any mistakes as you work. You will need to make sure that the area you are working on is fully protected and that you are using the correct equipment to apply the correct mix of paint to a surface.

Your speed in carrying out any tasks in a practice setting will also help to prepare you for the time set for the test. However, you must never rush the test! Always make sure you are working safely. Make sure throughout the test that you are wearing the appropriate PPE and using tools correctly.

Good luck!

CHECK YOUR KNOWLEDGE

1   Give one advantage of polythene dust sheets.
    a   they are available in different weights
    b   they do not absorb chemicals, such as paint stripper
    c   they present a professional image
    d   they remain in place when laid

2   What is a thixotropic paint?
    a   powder paint
    b   clear paint
    c   gel paint
    d   water-based paint

3   Why are water-based paint coatings becoming more popular?
    a   because they prevent rust
    b   because they have a stronger colour than solvent-based coatings
    c   because they do not give off strong fumes
    d   because they dry more quickly than solvent-based coatings

4   Which of these is a disadvantage of alkyd gloss paint?
    a   it does not provide a high-gloss finish.
    b   it does not have good covering power.
    c   it becomes brittle with age, leading to cracking and flaking
    d   it does not provide a good waterproof barrier

5   What is an achromatic colour?
    a   a warm colour
    b   a cool colour
    c   a bright colour
    d   not actually a colour

6   Accent colours are used to lift or add punch to a colour scheme, therefore:
    a   a small quantity of an accent colour is added to the colour scheme
    b   a medium quantity of an accent colour is added to the colour scheme
    c   a large quantity of an accent colour is added to the colour scheme
    d   an extra large quantity of an accent colour is added to the colour scheme

7   When yellow is at the top, which part of the colour wheel represents a warm colour?
    a   top
    b   bottom
    c   left-hand side
    d   right-hand side

8   What do the letters H, S and V stand for in relation to colours?
    a   hard, Soft, Value
    b   hue, Sand, Value
    c   hard, Saturation, Value
    d   hue, Saturation, Value

9   In the BS 4800 series, what range of colours does the number 00 represent?
    a   reds
    b   yellows
    c   purple/blues
    d   neutrals

10 In the code 10 E 53 from the BS 4800 series of paint colours, what does the 10 represent?
    a   hue
    b   greyness
    c   weight
    d   none of the above

UNIT 2021

Know how to apply standard papers to walls and ceilings

Wallpaper is one aspect of interior design. It is normally used to cover and decorate interior walls and ceilings of homes, offices, restaurants, doctors' surgeries, public houses (bars) and other buildings. Wallpaper can also be used as a centrepiece on a wall (wallpaper framed to look like a picture), to decorate panels on interior doors, and to brighten up the interior of cupboards and recesses under stairwells.

This unit will look at the techniques used for hanging wallpaper, mixing adhesives and applying papers.

This unit contains material that supports NVQ unit QCF 336 Hang wallcoverings (standard papers).

This unit also contains material that supports TAP Unit Hang wallcoverings (standard papers).

This unit will cover the following learning outcomes:

■ Describing methods used in wallpaper production
■ Selecting and preparing adhesives
■ Applying papers to ceilings and walls
■ Storing materials

K1. Describing methods used in wallpaper production

Figure 21.1 Wallpaper imitating a tapestry

Wallpaper was first used in the 1500s, but before that tapestries were hung on the walls in the homes of wealthier people and there were cheaper woollen or canvas hangings in the homes of the less well-off. These added colour to a room as well as providing an insulating layer between the stone walls and the interior of the room. These tapestries and the finer silks that were to follow were the forerunners of today's wallcoverings.

Figure 21.2 Tapestries are a feature still in some modern homes

Methods of production and printing for wallpaper

Wallpaper has long had an important role in decorative schemes, as the choice of wallpaper can influence the choice of other furnishings in the room. For much of its history, wallpaper has been more than merely printed paper at an affordable price. It has been designed to imitate items such as tapestry, velvet, chintz, silk drapery, linen, wood and masonry.

Production

Wallpapers are produced in many different ways. There are three types of wallpaper that you may come across in your career as a decorator:

- dry embossed paper
- wet embossed paper
- heat expansion paper.

Dry embossed paper

Dry embossed papers get their name because the paper used during production has been pressed into a relief mould or texture to create a hollowed out pattern on the reverse side of the wallpaper. This means when it is pasted to a surface the facing side of the paper will stand out prominently from the surface.

To produce these types of papers the printed wallpaper is passed through a steel embossing roller and a soft roller to press the pattern into the paper. Another method is passing the paper between two rollers, one with the pattern prominent (sticking out) and one having the same pattern sunken in (hollowed out), which produces a dry embossed paper.

Wet embossed wallpaper

To produce wet embossed wallpaper the method is very similar but it is produced in a wet state. The wet method helps it to retain its shape as these types of embossed papers are used for panels to imitate brickwork, stonework or timber. This produces supaglypta wallpaper, which is a heavy type of Anaglypta® (see page 172) and comes in various textures. During production a thicker and heavier type of paper is used and while in a wet state it is moulded between a steel roller and a special rubber coated printed roller to produce the texture.

Heat expansion paper

Heat expansion papers are similar to embossed papers. However, these wallpapers such as 'expanded vinyl', are papers that have a three-dimensional effect to them and are produced differently from normal embossed wallpaper. To produce these types of wallpapers an expanding agent (chemical) is added to liquid vinyl during manufacturing. This makes the wallpaper expand in size after it has been heated at high temperatures at the end of production. These types of wallpapers provide unique and dramatic appearances and still retain their three-dimensional effect after being hung on surfaces.

Ready-pasted paper

Another wallpaper you may come across is 'ready-pasted paper'. This is modern vinyl wallpaper which has paste already applied to it. You need a trough of water to be able to hang this paper; the trough is usually provided with a batch of wallpaper. To apply this paper you immerse the required length into the water and leave for the recommended time, then fold as required and apply immediately to the surface. (Many decorators normally mix a thin solution of paste then apply to the paper as normal, then hang the paper as this gives a better grip to the paper and is easier to handle.)

Remember, wallpaper will only look good on a surface if that surface has been prepared properly and the paper been applied correctly.

Did you know?

Low relief anaglypta type papers are created by dry embossing and are referred to as embossed papers. These are the cheapest and most common. Duplex papers (two papers bonded together) and anaglypta (pattern free/ brilliant white) are types of dry embossed paper.

Figure 21.3 Borders and friezes can help 'balance' a room

Appearance of patterns and paper types

Wallpaper is available in several different types of pattern:

- **Straight match** – a wallpaper design that is repeated horizontally across the paper
- **Drop match** – a wallpaper pattern that is repeated but with a space between the matches, as recommended by the manufacturers
- **Free match** – a wallpaper where there is no set match and therefore can be hung in any order and will look correct when hung. Stripe paper is a good example of this type of paper.

Basic wallpapers

Basic wallpapers are made from either:

- wood pulp
- vinyl.

Wood-pulp papers

Wood-pulp papers can be used as preparatory papers or finish papers.

Preparatory papers are usually painted with emulsion to provide a finish or they can be used as a base underneath finish papers. The different types of preparatory papers include:

- plain, coloured and reinforced lining paper
- wood chip
- Anaglypta®.

Finish papers are available in a variety of patterns:

- standard
- washable
- **embossed**.

> **Did you know?**
>
> Borders can be positioned anywhere in a room but you must remember that these papers are no different from standard papers – apart from being on a smaller scale – and therefore need to be matched if necessary and hung the same way as standard papers for example, plumb, level, etc.

> **Key term**
>
> **Embossed** – decorated with designs that stand out from the surface

Figure 21.4 Lining paper

Figure 21.5 Standard patterned wood-pulp paper

Vinyl wallpapers

There are three basic categories of vinyl paper:

- standard patterned vinyl
- sculptured vinyl
- blown vinyl, which can be either a patterned finish paper or a preparatory paper requiring painting.

Specialist surface coverings

Specialist coverings are those which are slightly different or unusual in some way from the standard papers already covered. They will probably only be used on particular jobs and in specific circumstances. Examples of specialist papers include the following.

- **Cloth-backed vinyl** – a paper that has a cotton backing and which is textured to look like fabric. Usually used in high-traffic areas such as halls, corridors and public places.
- **Lincrusta**® – a paper with a raised pattern or design that simulates carved plaster and wood. Usually used below dado rails, in pubs and restaurants and on staircases.
- **Paper-backed hessian** – a fabric surface covering made from **jute**. Usually used as a decorative finish in offices and public buildings.
- **Metal foil paper** – a surface covering with a metal finish. Usually used as a very decorative covering on feature walls.

Figure 21.6 Standard patterned vinyl paper

Figure 21.7 Sculptured vinyl paper

Figure 21.8 Patterned blown vinyl paper

Key term

Jute – a rough fibre made from a tropical plant

Figure 21.9 Cloth-backed vinyl paper

Figure 21.10 Lincrusta®

Figure 21.11 Paper-backed hessian

Figure 21.12 Metal foil paper

Lining paper A smooth preparatory paper available in a range of grades. Usually off-white, but brown and red lining papers are available as a base for coloured finish papers.	**Uses:** As a base for finish papers of even porosity or as a base for painting. Masks minor surface defects and is especially suitable for well-prepared surfaces. **Suitable wallpaper paste:** Starch or cellulose **Preparation and hanging:** Paste and allow paper to become supple before hanging. If used as a preparatory paper, it is usually hung horizontally to avoid the edges of the lining paper and finish paper falling in the same place. **Other information:** Available in 400, 600, 800 and 1000 grades in 200 mm and 555 mm wide single, double, triple or quad rolls.
Non-woven lining paper Made from cellulose and polyester fibre. Most common weight is 150 g.	**Uses:** On surfaces that may move, such as tongue and grooved cladding or badly-cracked plaster. **Suitable wallpaper paste:** Starch or tub paste **Preparation and hanging:** No need to soak. The wall can sometimes be pasted instead of the paper.
Patterned pulp paper A flat, standard wallpaper made from wood pulp, with a design printed on the surface. Many different qualities available ranging from simple machine-printed wallpaper to expensive hand-printed wallpaper.	**Uses:** General living areas such as living rooms, bedrooms and staircases. **Suitable wallpaper paste:** Cellulose **Preparation and hanging:** Check batch numbers and shade prior to hanging. **Other information:** Some patterned pulps have a coating of PVA varnish and are known as 'washables' because they can be sponged to remove stains.
Anaglypta® textured paper A brand name for an embossed paper made from wood pulp. A preparatory paper which requires painting.	**Uses:** Ceilings and walls in domestic premises. Masks minor surface defects. **Suitable wallpaper paste:** Starch paste, cellulose (thick) **Preparation and hanging:** Over-soaking, over-brushing joints and the use of seam rollers. will flatten the embossed pattern. Always leave a hairline gap at the joints, which can later be flooded with paint to provide an invisible joint. **Other information:** Can be used as an alternative to blown vinyl (see below).
Vinyl paper Made from a PVC (type of plastic) layer joined to a pulp backing paper. A very hard-wearing wallpaper.	**Uses:** Domestic and commercial premises where there is heavy human traffic. Kitchens, bathrooms or areas where there is condensation. **Suitable wallpaper paste:** Cellulose can be used, but tub paste is a better choice. Overlap adhesive is required on overlaps. Ready-pasted paper is widely available. **Preparation and hanging:** Always read the manufacturer's instructions. Can be smoothed out with a smoothing brush or a caulking tool. Stanley knives and a straight edge can be used to speed up the trimming process. **Other information:** Can be sponged to remove marks and stains. Can be peeled off and is easy to strip.
Blown vinyl paper A textured layer of PVC-bonded paper. There are two basic types: a textured preparatory paper that can be used as an alternative to Anaglypta® which needs to be painted and a textured and coloured finish paper that can be used as an alternative to embossed, patterned pulp.	**Uses:** Domestic and commercial premises. Not suitable in areas with heavy human traffic because the relief design can be easily damaged. **Suitable wallpaper paste:** Cellulose can be used, but tub paste is a better choice. Overlap adhesive is required on overlaps. **Preparation and hanging:** Apply with a smoothing brush. Avoid overlaps on internal/external angles by back trimming (double cutting).

Table 21.1 Basic types of wallpaper   Continued

Cloth-backed vinyl Made of PVC on a cotton scrim backing. The vinyl is either printed with a pattern or self-coloured and textured to look like fabric.	**Trimming:** Knife and steel straight edge **Pasting:** Use an adhesive containing a fungicide as the vinyl is water resistant and the paste will not be able to dry out through the material. Paste the cloth either with brush, roller or spread with filling knife. Paste the wall. **Hanging:** Fold and hang to a plumb line and butt all joints. Use the rounded edge of a plastic squeegee to smooth the material and smooth out all air from behind. Excess paste will be squeezed out at the edges, which must be immediately rinsed off. Paste the wall just beyond the width of material. Offer up the material dry and smooth down with squeegee. Paste the next section of wall and place the next length slightly overlapping the previous length before smoothing down. Place straight edge in line with the centre of the overlap and cut through the two thicknesses using a trimming knife and a 'first time cut'. Lift up the edges and take out the trimmings, then 'liven' the edges with paste and smooth down to a butt joint. Special tools are available for cutting through the overlaps that do not require a straight edge. **Other information:** Has a repeated pattern that the decorator may need to match. Available in 30 m x 1 m wide rolls and can be purchased by the metre.

Table 21.1 Basic types of wallpaper (continued)

Lincrusta® Has a raised pattern or texture, which is created by rolling a putty-like substance onto a continuous reel of heavy cartridge paper. The putty is embossed onto the surface while the paper back remains flat. Textures commonly produced are hessian and wood in sheet and plank form. Requires painting after hanging.	**Trimming:** Knife and straight edge, undercut. **Pasting:** Use Lincrusta® glue. Paste on the paper back. **Hanging:** Cut into lengths with a little in excess. Sponge several lengths of the paper backing with warm (not hot) water and leave to soak for 15 to 20 minutes, which will cause the paper to expand and will prevent blisters in the finished work. After soaking, sponge off any water and cut the expanded length to fit exactly. Apply Lincrusta® glue to the backing. Hang with butt joints, smoothing down with a rubber roller using firm pressure and a vigorous action. When soaking and pasting, avoid sharp folds which may cause cracking of the surface. Lay lengths back-to-back when soaking which will help to retain moisture and achieve even expansion. External angles must be turned by cutting through the putty on the face (but not through the paper) exactly on the angle and bending the paper back around the angle. Any gaps on the angle can be filled with stiff linseed oil putty. Internal angles must be cut to fit exactly. **Painting:** The surface is slightly oily and greasy and must be wiped off with white spirit before painting with oil-based paint (not emulsion). **Other information:** Store rolls standing upright to avoid the weight cracking the face putty. Available in 1025 mm x 525 mm rolls; can also be supplied in panels and borders.
Woven glass fibre White glass fibre woven into three textures: coarse, medium and fine. Generally used to reinforce cracked and imperfect surfaces and is then painted.	**Trimming:** Knife and straight edge. Trim on wall. **Pasting:** Use PVA-reinforced paste or PVA adhesive (straight). Paste the wall. **Hanging:** Cut the lengths with 50 mm excess at top and bottom. Paste the wall evenly with a short pile paint roller, finishing a little short of the actual width of the glass fibre so that the edges of the first and second lengths overlap in a completely dry state. Hang the dry fabric and smooth down with a felt roller or plastic squeegee. Paste the second section of wall, again finishing a little short of the actual width. Cut through the overlap with a knife and straight edge, peeling away the two edges. Brush paste onto the 'missed' stripe of wall and press the two trimmed edges down as a perfect butt joint. If the wall is pasted to the full width of glass fibre then the edges will take in water and become too wet to obtain crisp, clean cutting, resulting in ragged joints. Trim the fabric to parallel widths on the pasteboard. Paste the wall to the entire width of the fabric. Hang dry, trimmed fabric, smoothing down with a felt roller. Paste the next section of wall surface and hang the next length of dry, trimmed fabric with a butt joint. Continue with the next length using the same method. **Other information:** Available in 50 m x 1 m rolls and can be purchased by the metre.

Table 21.2 Specialist surface coverings

Continued

Paper-backed felt Made from a thick blanket of dyed short wool fibres.	**Trimming:** Knife and straight edge. The main problem is making a first cut. If a blunt knife or not enough pressure is used, a second cut can make the edges very ragged. A clean cut first time gives perfect butt joints. **Pasting:** Use stiff tub paste or PVA-reinforced adhesive. Paste the paper back. **Hanging:** Very little soaking is required after pasting and folding the material. Hang to a plumb line with butt joints, smoothing down with a felt roller. Reverse alternate lengths to minimise the effect of any edge-to-edge shading. Angles can be turned in the normal way. If the fabric and paper are not too wet, cutting to top and bottom and around obstacles can be done with a template and knife. If paper-backed felt is too wet, either allow to dry off and then cut with a template and knife, or mark with template and chalk and then cut with scissors. **Other information:** Avoid getting paste on the cloth, which can damage it! Available in 50 m × 0.91 m rolls and can be purchased by the metre.
Paper-backed hessian Made of jute, which can be dyed and then woven, or woven into cloth and then dyed. Laminated onto a paper back.	**Trimming:** Knife and straight edge. The key to hanging hessian is clean first-time cutting when trimming the material. If a blunt knife or insufficient pressure is used and a second cut has to be taken, then the edges can become frayed. Two slightly frayed edges look very unsightly when butt jointed. Clean, first-time cutting hides the joint perfectly. **Pasting:** Use stiff tub paste or PVA-reinforced paste. Paste the paper back. **Hanging:** Very little soaking is necessary after pasting and folding the material. Hang to a plumb line while smoothing down with a felt roller. Reverse alternate lengths to minimise the effect of any edge-to-edge shading. Angles can be turned in the normal way. If the fabric and paper are not too wet, cutting to top and bottom and around obstacles can be done with a template and knife. If too wet, either allow to dry off before cutting, or mark with template and chalk and cut with scissors. **Other information:** Avoid getting paste on the cloth, which can damage it! Available in 50 m x 0.91 m rolls and can be purchased by the metre.
Paper-backed laminated foils A surface covering made from several thin layers, namely: paper (as the backing), a metal or mirror-like finish (foil) and a laminated top layer.	**Trimming:** Knife and straight edge. Undercut slightly. **Pasting:** Some foils are straightforward laminates of tarnished metal leaves, or figured and engraved continuous sheets applied onto a paper backing. These present no problem when pasted and hung in the normal way except for a curling of the edges similar to cork veneer papers. See type 1 foils below. Other foils with burnished mirror-like backgrounds present many problems. The mirror-like background magnifies every tiny defect behind the foil so preparation must be perfect. If the foil backing is pasted, even the paste brush marks can damage the finish. Paste must be applied evenly to the wall with a short pile paint roller and the stipple effect allowed to flow out before offering up the dry material. See type 2 foils. *Type 1 foils*: Paste the material. *Type 2 foils*: Paste the wall once or twice with PVA adhesive (must contain a fungicide). Some highly reflective foils are also laminated to include a plastic membrane – these curl badly if pasted. Even when dry they are very stiff and the curl from the roll will not lie flat. Use a very sticky adhesive to hold this type of foil. This can be achieved by pasting the wall twice. **Hanging** *Type 1 foils*: Fold down without creasing, then hang to a plumb line and butt all joints. Smooth down with felt or rubber roller. Cut to top and bottom and around obstacles in the normal way with scissors. *Type 2 foils*: Paste the wall once or twice as necessary, allow stipple texture to flow out and hang the dry foil to a plumb line, then butt all joints. Smooth down with felt or rubber roller. Cut to top and bottom and around obstacles with plastic template and knife. Remove any paste immediately from the surface after fixing with a soft sponge, and polish dry with a very soft cloth. **Other information** Available in 7.31 m × 0.91 m rolls.

Table 21.2 Specialist surface coverings (continued)

Continued

Advantages	Disadvantages
Inexpensive	Less adhesive than starch paste
Little risk of staining	Can cause paper to over-expand, resulting in wrinkling or mismatch
Easy to apply	If used on wallpaper that is unable to let water pass through it, such as vinyl, the water content in the adhesive may be prevented from drying out through the paper, leading to damage
Easy to mix	
Does not rot and can remain useable for a long time	
Contains a fungicide to prevent mould growth	

Table 21.5 Advantages and disadvantages of cellulose adhesive

Adhesives designed for specific wall coverings

- **Border adhesive** – is ideal for applying vinyl on vinyl, for example when applying a border paper on top of another paper. It has strong adhesive properties.
- **Lincrusta®** – glue is a very strong adhesive with good bonding properties.
- **Overlap adhesive** – is designed for bonding vinyl to vinyl. It can be used on vinyl to bond overlaps on internal/external angles and to apply border paper over vinyl.

Factors that may affect the consistency of adhesives

Table 21.6 shows some of the key factors that can affect the consistency of adhesives.

Incorrect preparation	If this is not done correctly then the adhesive may not adhere, for example if the surface is not sealed or there is a covering of dust.
Paper type	Certain papers will need a different thickness of paste to enable the paper to adhere correctly. Instructions are always printed on the labels from the manufacturer.
Paper weight	As above, if papers are heavy and the paste/adhesive has not been mixed correctly then the paper could fall off the surface
Room temperature	If the temperature is not right then this will also affect the drying time of the adhesive and cause problems with paper peeling off.
Surface	If the surface has not been sealed then the adhesive could be absorbed into the surface. This means it could leave the paper before the correct drying time has been reached. This would then make the paper detach from the wall.

Table 21.6 Factors affecting consistency

Defects related to incorrect adhesive consistency

There are some common defects you will encounter if working with an adhesive with an incorrect consistency.

- **Delamination** – caused by a thin consistency and leaving wall coverings to soak too long. The paper will peel away from the backing.
- **Blistering** – the appearance of a 'blister' or 'bubble' in a surface covering. Caused by poor smoothing, over-brushing, uneven pasting, use of incorrect adhesive or the lining not adhering properly.
- **Stretching** – occurs if wallpaper has not been left to soak for the recommended time and the paper becomes overstretched on the wall. Can also be caused by the paper being forced into position after it has begun to adhere to the surface or by hanging the paper in position for long periods of time, such as matching up, prior to adhering it to the surface.

K3. Applying papers to ceilings and walls

Wallpaper is applied to walls and ceilings as well as archways, columns, sloping ceilings, staircases/stairwells and dormer window reveals. It is essential that you have the right training before you hang any wallpaper, as it is a complex task.

Factors to be considered when planning work

The following general good practice points should be followed when preparing a surface for wallpapering:

- Ensure the surface is sound, clean, dry and free from grease. Wallpaper will not stick to grease and dirt and it is also unhygienic to paper over dirty surfaces.
- Surfaces must be in good condition. Flaking paint should be rubbed down with medium abrasive sandpaper back to a firm surface, then sealed and filled. Powdery or crumbling surfaces should be painted with stabilising solution or PVA resin.
- Gloss or eggshell surfaces should be roughened with abrasive paper to provide a good key for the wallpaper paste.
- Prepared gloss surfaces can be covered with PVA adhesive to improve sticking.

- Any nail or screw heads must be primed with a metal primer to prevent rust staining.

We will now look at the preparation of some specific surfaces.

Painted surfaces

Preparing previously painted surfaces for wallpaper is very similar to the preparation required before applying paint. For further information, see Unit 2019 pages 97–129.

Bare plaster surfaces

Bare plaster surfaces should be **sized** with a purpose-made size or wallpaper adhesive or paste, such as cellulose paste or tub paste. Do not use starch paste to size plaster as this will flake when it dries, leaving an unsound surface.

Sizing is essential as it evens out the **porosity** of the bare plaster and prevents the water within wallpaper paste from being absorbed by the plaster. This is known as 'snatch' and, if it happens, the decorator will be unable to slide the wallpaper into position.

Some products, such as universal wall covering primer, are designed to allow the easy stripping of wallpaper when the room is next decorated. A thick coat of emulsion can also be used to size bare plaster.

New plaster must be allowed to dry out. Hard wall plaster may need up to six months to dry thoroughly before it is ready for wallpapering. Plasterboard that has been coated with board finish plaster (or skim) can be papered as soon as the plaster is visibly dry.

Plasterboard surfaces

If new plasterboard has been sized with a suitable adhesive or emulsion, the wallpaper will bond to the surface. However, removing the wallpaper at a later date could leave the paper surface of the plasterboard stripped or badly damaged. To avoid this, size the surface with an oil-based primer. This will make the paper surface of the plasterboard waterproof and less likely to suffer damage when paper is stripped from it. A wall covering primer can also be used.

If removing wallpaper from the surface, all traces of old paste and small pieces of wallpaper should be removed by using water and a paste brush and scrubbing the surface. A Scotch-Brite® pad can also be used to do this. Finally, use a sponge and some clean water to rinse off the surface.

Key terms

Sized – sealed

Porosity – the ability of a surface to allow water to pass through

Figure 21.14 Sizing will prevent plaster absorbing water from paste

> **Remember**
>
> Before hanging surface coverings, always read the manufacturer's instructions. These will contain all the information required to hang the wallpaper correctly, including soaking time, recommended paste and surface preparation required.

Preparing to apply surface coverings

You will need to lay down a dust sheet, mix the paste, erect the pasteboard and find a box for waste cuttings. All fixtures and fittings should be removed. Any exposed wires should be taped with insulation tape to prevent electric shock. Electrical fittings should be switched off at the mains and removed by a trained electrician. Relocate screws into the holes to make them easy to find when the wall is covered.

Time spent planning is important, because a well set-up room can save a lot of time and effort and can help you to use paper more economically. Remember that some wallpapers are very expensive, and the decorator is responsible for getting the preparation right.

The following golden rules should always be followed when preparing to apply surface coverings.

- Read the manufacturer's instructions supplied with each roll.
- Check each roll individually to ensure it is not damaged.
- Check that the batch numbers and shades are identical.
- Open the rolls to check the pattern and printing.
- Identify the pattern, for example straight match or drop match pattern.
- Check which way the paper should be applied. Some patterns are not easy to identify. If you are unsure, contact the client or the manufacturer.

If the wallpaper is a straight match, lengths of paper can be cut from one roll at a time. If the pattern is a drop match, cut your lengths from two rolls. This is because two lengths of a drop match patterned paper cut to the same size from the same roll cannot be used adjacent to each other on a wall because they would not match.

> **Remember**
>
> Measure twice but only cut once. In other words, double-check your measurements before making the cut.

To cut lengths from two rolls use the following procedure.

- place two rolls on the pasteboard.
- match the pattern at the edge using the two rolls.
- trim both top edges so that the waste is equal.
- label one roll A and the other B using a pencil on the back of each length. Keep on marking them alternately until all lengths are cut.
- keep the lengths in order when pasting and hanging.

When the first length of wallpaper has been measured and cut from the roll, it can be used as a template for cutting the other required lengths. After offering the first cut length up to the wall, check that there have not been any measuring errors. If not, all of the full lengths can then be cut. You are now ready to start pasting the lengths.

Reasons for marking lines

To hang your first length of wall covering – either to a wall area or a ceiling – you must have a straight line to work from to make sure the paper hangs straight.

Marking a plumb line

- Mark your plumb line only once it stops swinging.
- Make sure that the string is hanging freely – check it isn't snagged on anything.
- Use only one eye to sight the plumb line and continue to use the same eye for every mark you make.
- When marking your pencil line against the string, do not overstretch but move your head to the pencil and keep your aiming eye level to the mark that you are about to make.
- If you need to move your hand down the string, make sure that it does not move by using alternate hands to position the string.
- An alternative way to mark a plumb starting point is first to measure the area and decide where you want to start. Then, using a spirit level, draw a vertical line down the surface with a pencil from top to bottom – making sure that the spirit level is placed at your marking points throughout the process.

Considerations when cutting

- **Access equipment** – if papering a ceiling you will need to use staging to make the task easier and safe. You will need to consider step ladders to reach the tops of walls and use the correct access set up for staircases.
- **Light source** – try to make sure you work away from the light so the joints have less shadow on them. This is to avoid the light showing any papering joints and therefore spoiling the overall appearance of the finished job.
- **Room dimensions** – measure the room accurately to purchase the correct amount of wallpaper for the job.
- **Economy** – plan the papering correctly to avoid any costly wastage. If large patterns are being used make sure you maximise the wallpaper so little waste is created.

Figure 21.15 A plumb bob must be used accurately

Reasons for selecting folds

The paper should be allowed to soak before hanging, but to ensure **equal stretch** each length should have the same amount of soaking time. This can be done by working with two lengths at any one time, pasting one, then pasting the other before hanging the first length, and so on.

Now you are ready to fold a length of paper. How it is folded will depend on how long the length is or where it is to be hung.

- Two-lap fold – if the wallpaper is of normal room length, you should use a two-lap fold, making the top fold the longest fold. It should be roughly two-thirds to one-third.
- Concertina fold – this series of small folds can be easily unfolded during the paper hanging process. The concertina fold is normally used for papering ceilings or for applying paper horizontally. It can also be used for folding very long lengths before vertical application.

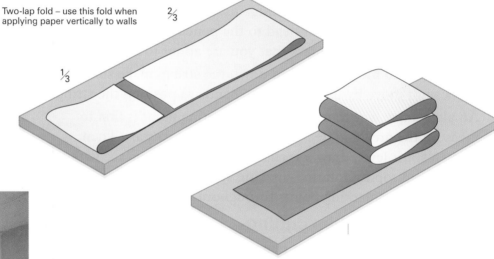

Two-lap fold – use this fold when applying paper vertically to walls

⅔

⅓

Concertina fold – use this fold when applying paper horizontally to walls or when papering ceilings

Figure 21.16 Types of wallpaper fold

Figure 21.17 Hanging paper vertically

Papering walls and ceilings

Papering vertically

Take the first length of wallpaper and offer it up to the plumb line, with the longest fold opened and then place it on the wall. You should be able to slide the paper accurately towards the plumb line. Smooth the paper down with the brush. Work from the centre towards the edges. When all the air is smoothed out, fold down the bottom fold and apply it to the wall as before.

Papering a ceiling

Make a chalk line on the ceiling to work from, to ensure the first length is straight. Always use a concertina fold and, after soaking the paper, offer up the first length to the ceiling against a line that allows for a 20 mm overlap at the wall edge. The concertina folds should be around 350 mm per fold. Apply one fold to the ceiling while supporting the unopened folds with a **decorator's crutch**. Smooth out the first fold. Then open one more fold and repeat the process – do not try to apply more than one fold at a time. When free of air pockets and creases, the paper should be trimmed out to both wall edges.

> **Remember**
>
> Smooth out wallpaper from the centre to the edge. This pushes any air bubbles to the edge and out from the surface.

Chalk line

Apply the first length to the ceiling using the chalk line as guidance and leave an overlap at the wall edge

Smooth out the first fold, then open and apply the next length

> **Key term**
>
> **Decorator's crutch** – a rolled-up length of wallpaper or a piece of wood used to support a concertina fold

Figure 21.18 Papering a ceiling

Hanging paper around a window

Hang the paper on one side of the window (see 1 in Figure 21.19), making a cut that allows some of the paper to be folded around the reveal. Next, hang paper above and below the window, ensuring that they are plumb (see 2 and 3). Now patch the underside of the reveal in the corner (4). Allow approximately 10 mm of paper to overlap (see dotted lines). Repeat this process for the other side of the window. If the window is particularly wide, you may want to mark a plumb line to make sure that the next full length of paper after the window is straight.

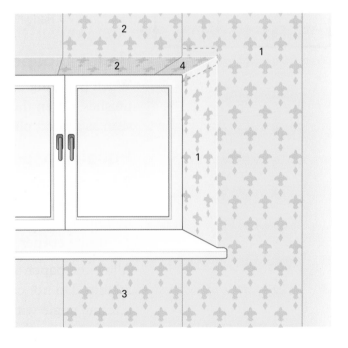

Figure 21.19 Hanging paper round a window

Hanging paper up a staircase

When applying paper to a staircase always start with the longest drop (length). After applying this first length, work from either side of it.

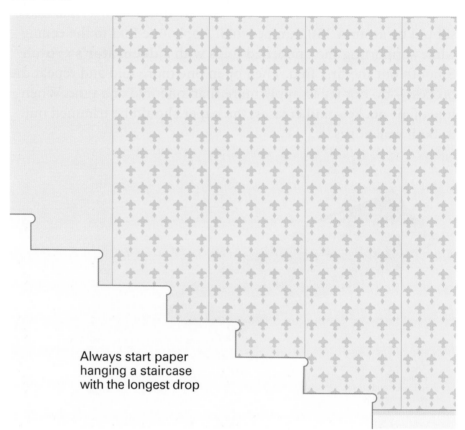

Always start paper hanging a staircase with the longest drop

Figure 21.20 Hanging paper up a staircase

Hanging paper around a door

When papering a room you need to have an area where the paper finishes. Often the point chosen for this is behind a door. This is seen as a good place to finish as it is usually hidden from view.

Hanging paper around internal and external angles

When papering around an external or internal angle, the same method is applied with the plumb line. When the paper needs to go round an internal angle, never use one length to wrap around the inside corner – always do it in two lengths.

Allow the paper to go around the inside corner by no more than 25 mm. Do not carry on papering around an inside corner or internal angle with an existing length as you will cause the paper to start to spring off and it will not keep straight. It is most likely you will have to use and cut one length and piece them back together. To do this measure the space between the edge of the existing length and the internal corner, remembering to add an extra 25 mm to go round the internal angle.

With the remaining paper, measure the distance needed to paper back into the corner. Start again with a plumb bob to mark your straight line, then hang the strip and make sure that you paper into the internal angle, covering up the 25 mm edge. If you are using a patterned paper, you will need to match it up as well as you can.

The same method is applied to paper around an external angle. However you need to allow the paper to wrap around the external angle by at least 50 mm. Then, as before, start again with a plumb line and cover up the 50 mm paper so your lengths hang straight.

Hanging paper around an inside corner

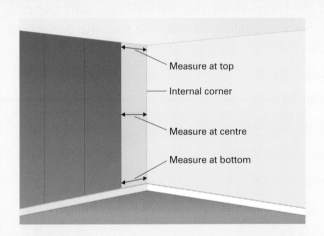

- Measure at top
- Internal corner
- Measure at centre
- Measure at bottom

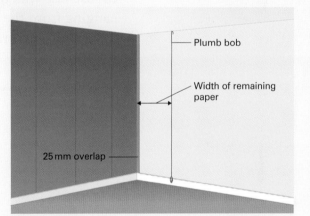

- Plumb bob
- Width of remaining paper
- 25 mm overlap

Step 1: Measure the space between the existing length and the internal corner. Cut the next length of paper to fit this space with an additional 25 mm for an overlap.

Step 2: After pasting the first length, measure the width needed for the remaining paper from the internal corner and mark your straight line. Paper the corner, covering the overlap.

Centralising a patterned wallpaper

Figure 21.21 shows a chimney breast and alcoves of a room papered with a patterned wallpaper. The wallpaper has a set pattern and the pattern match is horizontally set – it does not drop. The wallpaper has been centralised – that means that the first length of wallpaper has been placed in the centre of the chimney breast. Notice how this creates a balanced effect.

Did you know?

Although it is not desirable, a slight mismatch in the corner is not normally visible or noticed and quite often is unavoidable.

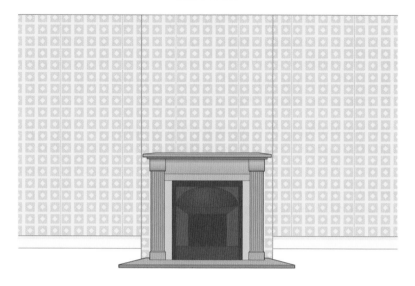

Figure 21.21 Centralising patterned wallpaper on a chimney breast

Key term

Focal point – a place where your eyes will tend to look

The chimney breast is a **focal point** of a room and can be the place to start papering if the whole room is to be papered in the same patterned paper. If a room does not have a chimney breast, choose one wall of the room as the feature wall and start paper hanging from the centre of that wall to ensure that the pattern of the paper is centralised.

Papering round an archway

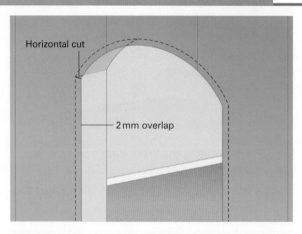

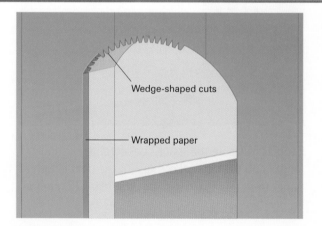

Step 1: Paper the walls on both sides of the archway, allowing a 20 to 30 mm overlap at the perimeter of the arch.

Step 2: Next, make a series of small cuts (every 20 to 30 mm) in from the edge of the overlap – this is so you can fold the wallpaper onto the underside of the arch.

Cut a strip of paper to fit the underside of the arch, leaving a few millimetres at each end of the length. Paste and apply to the underside of the arch. If you are using a patterned paper, cut two lengths for the underside of the arch and overlap them in the middle, then splice them through the middle to hide your joint.

Sockets, switches and ceiling roses

When you encounter any sockets or switches you will need to place the paper over the switch or socket and gently poke your shears or knife through the middle of where the socket or switch is located, then cut outwards towards each corner of the item. The next step is to smooth the paper into the socket or switch. After you have done this, trim the paper and leave about 10 mm at each edge.

Loosen the screws holding the item in place and push the paper behind to hide any edges then retighten the screws. Clean away any excess paste left on the surface of the sockets or switches to leave a clean job.

Remember

This technique of cutting paper is known as a star cut. A half star cut is used when only half the paper lands on the ceiling rose.

Papering round a ceiling rose

Step 1 Brush the first strip of paper over the rose.

Step 2 Use scissors to make small triangular cuts in the paper towards the edge of the rose.

Step 3 Use a knife to trim off the small triangular pieces, then smooth down the paper.

Step 4 Place the next length of paper over the rose to get an impression on the paper. Cut out the impression but leave about 50mm (2") overhang at the edge of the ceiling rose. Make small triangular cuts towards the edge of the paper, then trim off the pieces and smooth down the paper.

Know how to apply standard papers to walls and ceilings **Unit 2021**

Remember

All centre pieces vary so careful planning is always recommended.

Functional skills

In answering the questions in this section, you are practising the functional skills required to read different texts and take appropriate action, e.g. respond to advice/instructions. **FE 1.2.1 – 1.2.3** This may also involve giving oral answers to questions from your tutor and is practise for speaking and listening – **FE 1.1.1 – FE 1.1.4**.

Communicating effectively is an essential skill in everyday work. You may be asked to take part in discussions about your work and asked for your opinions.

If the centre piece is larger then you would have to make sure that you plan the papering correctly by using one length to cover half the centre piece then cut and trim into place then apply the next length across the other half and repeat the process.

Why lining is used

Lining is a base for finishing papers of even porosity or as a base for painting. It can mask minor surface defects and is suitable for well-prepared surfaces. It is also used for masking – or making good – damage to walls and surfaces where filling and sanding has not resolved the defects prior to applying paints.

Lining paper can also be used to hide strong-coloured walls prior to repainting them in a lighter coloured paint or repapering them with lighter coloured wallpaper. The use of the right grade of lining paper hides any imperfections on the wall and is ideal as a base for hanging wallcoverings. It is also advisable to hang lining paper on solvent-painted walls to give a more absorbent surface for wallpapers to adhere to.

Working life

Steve and Jakob are finishing off their apprenticeship and are working for a local decorating firm. They have been given the task of wallpapering a staircase for a client. The charge hand Michelle is assisting the two apprentices. The client wants a drop pattern paper applied to the staircase. Michelle has explained to the client that using this type of paper will be costly and she has asked Steve and Jakob to organise some ladders, step ladders and staging planks for the task.

Is Michelle right to advise the client about the cost implications of using drop pattern paper on a staircase? Is the scaffold equipment suitable for this type of work? You will need to think about the type of access equipment you might need in this situation. Where will the first length of paper be hung from? You will need to think about the first job the apprentices will need to do and what sequence should be used to apply the paper. What type of wallpaper would be suitable for a staircase? What risks are involved with papering a staircase? Is this type of work suitable for Steve and Jakob to do during their apprenticeship?

Methods for calculating quantity of paper

There are two main methods of calculating how much wallpaper you will require.

Girthing method

Use a roll of wallpaper as width guide to measure the number of full lengths required. Mark where each width will appear along the area to be papered and repeat this method until you have gone across the whole area. Then measure the height of the wall to see how many full lengths can be cut from a single roll of wallpaper. This is called the girthing method and can be used to measure an area quickly. However, remember that miscalculations may cause you to run out of paper during application.

Area method

Measure up a room or take dimensions from a drawing. To measure up for a room you will need to measure each wall area separately. Measure the width/length and height of each wall area then multiply together to get the area which needs papering. This also applies to the ceiling area as well. Add together to calculate the total surface area of the room, including windows and doors. Finally, work out the area of the off takes (things that will not be papered, such as the doors and windows) and subtract this amount from the total surface area. This will give you the surface area that requires papering. Then divide the total surface area (of the room) by the surface area of the wallpaper roll. This method is time-consuming, but more accurate.

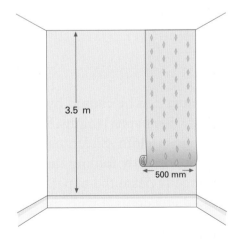

Method 1 – Girthing method – use the width of a roll of wallpaper and measure the height of the wall

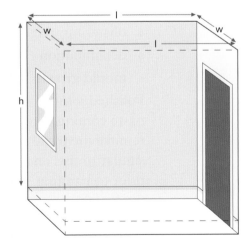

Method 2 – Area method – calculate the total surface area of the room and then subtract the off takes (e.g. doors and windows)

Figure 21.22 Working out wallpaper quantities

Cutting considerations

When hanging any type of wallpaper it is important that you cut it correctly to avoid any mistakes. There are several key considerations you need to make when cutting.

- **Type of pattern and pattern match** – bold, prominent and small repeating patterns play a major role in cutting lengths correctly. After selecting your starting point, and choosing a suitable **header** on the paper's pattern, match up your subsequent lengths making sure the pattern matches together and you have enough lengths of paper to cover the width of the wall you selected to start from. Usually it is best to match your paper up on your paste table prior to any pasting and then cut and number each length before hanging.

- **Wastage** – a straight or set pattern will not usually have a lot of wastage due to the number of repeating areas. An offset or drop pattern will have fewer places in which the pattern will match correctly, therefore you must make sure you position and match the paper with as little wastage as possible.

- **Batch numbers and shading of the paper** – always check each roll has the same batch number and code before opening. The paper may need reversing due to shading.

Faults and defects caused by careless pasting

Many of the faults that can be caused by careless pasting have been covered earlier in this unit and in previous units. For more information turn to the following pages:

- blistering (page 180)
- delamination (page 180)
- mould growth (page 122).

Polished joints on the face of the paper can be caused by excess paste coming through the joints between paper lengths. You must remove the paste with a damp sponge or cloth. Sheen patches are similar to this and are caused by not correctly folding the paper prior to hanging. To avoid this, correctly paste the paper and fold the lengths prior to hanging to avoid any contact with the face of the paper. Remove any paste on the decorative side.

Key term

Header – this is where you will have a point picked out on the paper for example, a large flower head, and need that same flower head running horizontally across the room

Defects caused by careless handling and planning

These defects include the following:

- **Loss of emboss** – occurs when too much pressure is placed on the face of the paper after application to the surface.
  When smoothing and removing air bubbles, too much pressure can flatten the pattern, losing definition and spoiling the effect.
- **Shading** – certain papers need to be reversed as they have been manufactured with a slight shading difference.
  If instructions are not followed there will be a shade area on the paper, which will stand out after application.
- **Inaccurate angle cutting** – results in paper being cut too short and being useless for the job and needing replacing.
  Angles must be worked out to make sure there is enough excess paper left to trim into reveals.

Reasons for following pasting methods

There are some methods that can be used to speed up pasting for large jobs.

- **Pasting machines** – have a supply of paste ready in a reservoir attached to the machine, allowing multiple lengths to soak and then be hung in succession. They save time during application, but are more time-consuming to clean and store.
- **Rollers** – can speed up manual application of paste, but can become messy if not used correctly.
- **Ready-pasted papers** – have an adhesive applied to them during manufacturing and are designed to be submerged in a water trough then applied to the surface. This avoids pasting the paper. However, this method is messy and can become difficult to apply; it is used far less now than when it was first manufactured.

Good pasting technique

- Stand in front of the pasteboard and place the length of paper on the pasteboard reverse side upwards.
- Move the furthest edge just over the edge of the pasteboard.
- Apply paste down the centre of the cut length.
- Keep applying the paste from the centre to the furthest edge. Do not go from edge to centre because the paste will drop onto the face side of the paper.
- Move the cut length so the nearest edge is just over the edge of the pasteboard and continue to work the paste brush from centre to edge, not from edge to centre.

Figure 21.23 A good pasting technique

Appropriate use of shears, knife and straight edge when trimming waste

When trimming excess wallpaper at ceilings and skirting boards your cutting must be correct and careful. There are a number of ways to trim the wallpaper after application. A common method is to place a straight edge or caulk board against the meeting point between the ceiling and the wall and then use a craft knife and slice through the paper along the whole width, taking care not to tear the paper. You can also use a casing wheel.

Another method is to firmly press the paper into the meeting point between the ceiling and wall with the back of your paperhanging shears and either draw a faint pencil line at this point or simply crease the paper into shape and then peel back the paper. Use your shears to trim the excess paper off, remembering to take your time to avoid any miss-cuts.

Remember

With all these methods you would need to clean the blades thoroughly to remove excess paste that could cause your equipment to clog up and therefore damage the paper.

K4. Storing materials

We have covered the storage of materials in several earlier units. Refer back to Unit 1001 pages 12–15, Unit 2003 pages 92–93 and Unit 2020 pages 143–47 for more information.

Wallpaper rolls must be stored in racks with their ends protected from damage. They should also be stored in batches with their identifying number

Figure 21.24 Correct storage of wallpaper

clearly marked. They should not be overstacked, which could cause damage. Rolls should be kept wrapped and protected from dust and they should never be in direct sunlight, which can result in fading of colours. Dry conditions are necessary to prevent mould growth. Some special wall coverings have a shelf life that should be taken into consideration.

FAQ

Do I have to plumb a line when papering vertically – can I not just start from a corner of the room?

It is important to plumb a line when papering in order to make sure that your paper is hanging straight and does not run off and cause problems, especially when using patterned papers. If you start from a corner of a room it is very likely that the paper will run off. This is because most walls will not be perfectly plumb. Therefore if you use a plumb bob and line, or a straight edge and spirit level, you can always be sure that your wallpaper covering will hang straight.

Why should I check that all the wallpaper rolls have the same batch number on them if they all look the same colour or pattern anyway?

Although the paper may look the same, if the batch numbers are not identical the paper may be shaded differently and will therefore show up and look odd after the paper has been applied to the area. It would have to be removed and the whole job started again.

Check it out

1 Describe three different types of wallpaper and explain their different uses, stating what factors might decide which you choose to use.

2 Explain why it is important to check the batch numbers on wallpapers, giving reasons why these might be different.

3 Describe three main types of adhesive that you could use and explain where and when you may use these for wallpapering.

4 Prepare a method statement to explain the process that needs to be followed in order to make sure a surface is prepared and ready for the application of wallpaper.

5 Explain what can be applied to plasterboard prior to papering to protect it from damage.

6 Using diagrams and sketches, explain the processes that must be followed to hang paper horizontally and vertically.

7 Using a room in the building where you work, put together a plan for repapering this room, taking into account the different obstacles you will need to work around and making a calculation of the amount of paper you will need to use. Make sure that you take into account the possibility of wastage.

8 Explain the reasons behind marking lines when hanging paper, and describe some the main methods used to complete this work.

9 Name four different types of common surface defect and explain how each may be caused. Explain the methods that can be used to prevent these.

10 Prepare a method statement explaining the best pasting method to be used for a wall in your building.

Getting ready for assessment

The information contained in this unit, as well as continued practical assignments that you will carry out in your college or training centre, will help you in preparing for both your end-of-unit test and the diploma multiple-choice test. It will also aid you in preparing for the work that is required for the synoptic practical assignments.

You will often have to work with a variety of different papers that need to be placed for decoration on walls. To do this correctly you will need to know about the different adhesives you can use, as well as the different types of wallpapers that can be produced. Your practical work will require you to use this knowledge to apply lining, wood grain and non-matching papers to walls in a range of situations.

You will need to be familiar with:

- describing methods used in wallpaper production
- selecting and preparing adhesives
- applying papers to ceilings and walls
- storing materials.

For learning outcome three you will need to be able to explain the factors considered when planning the application of papers to a range of different surfaces and around a range of obstructions. You will need to be able to select, position and erect the appropriate access equipment and select the correct tools and equipment in order to complete the work. When working with surfaces you will need to be able to calculate, using girthing and area methods, the correct quantities of pattern types, then shading, measuring and cutting batches of lengths with the minimum wastage of paper. For hanging paper, you will need to be able to measure and mark lines to hang to and paste paper without misses, folding lengths and soaking and taking into account pasting factors. You will always need to be sure that you apply papers using correct processes, matching areas and avoiding defects. As always, you need to be sure that you are working to current health and safety regulations.

Before you carry out any work, think of a plan of action, which will tell you the order in which you need to do things. It will also record a rough timescale for the work you need to carry out, in order to make sure that you complete everything you need to do safely. You will need to refer back to this plan at each stage to make sure that you are not making any mistakes as you work. Applying foundation and plain papers to a range of surface areas is a crucial practical skill for painters and decorators and you will need to be sure that you are following all the correct procedures to make sure the final job is completed to the highest possible standard.

Your speed in carrying out any tasks in a practice setting will also help to prepare you for the time set for the test. However, you must never rush the test! Always make sure you are working safely. Make sure throughout the test that you are wearing the appropriate PPE and using tools correctly.

Good luck!

CHECK YOUR KNOWLEDGE

1 It is essential to size bare plaster surfaces before applying wallpaper, in order to prevent:
a the water in the paste causing stains on the wallpaper
b the water in the paste being absorbed by the plaster
c damage to the surface when the wallpaper is removed
d the plaster from drying out

2 When calculating the amount of wallpaper required, a decorator usually allows a wastage of:
a 5%
b 10%
c 15%
d 20%

3 What sort of fold should you use for wallpaper which will be hung vertically?
a concertina folds
b two-lap folds
c double folds
d 1:2 folds

4 What is a decorator's crutch used for?
a supporting concertina folds when applying paper to a ceiling
b supporting a paintbrush when applying paint to a ceiling
c supporting the decorator when working at height
d none of the above

5 What common surface covering defect can be caused by underlying dampness?
a blistering
b staining
c peeling
d embossing

6 Where would you start paperhanging in a room which has a window and a fireplace built within it?
a the window wall
b the fireplace wall
c the wall opposite the window
d the wall opposite the fireplace

7 What type of wallpaper is best suited for a room that has a lot of condensation?
a Lincrusta®
b blown vinyl
c lining paper
d vinyl paper

8 If you fail to let the wallpaper soak for the recommended time during paperhanging what defect will occur?
a paper will blister/bubble up on the wall
b paper will shrink on the wall
c paper will lift from the wall
d all of the above

9 What does the international performance symbol →|← represent on wallpaper information?
a drop match
b straight match
c random match
d none of the above

10 When papering a ceiling, which is the best place to start from?
a from the window wall
b the centre of the ceiling
c from the fireplace wall
d any of the above

UNIT 2022

Know how to produce specialist decorative finishes 2

The way that paint is applied to a surface can produce some interesting and decorative features. Special effects, such as texture, pattern and the illusion of a different surface can all be created by a skilled decorator using the contents of their tool box. In this unit you will learn about the different methods and techniques used to create a wide range of decorative finishes.

This unit contains material that supports NVQ units QCF 333 Apply paint systems by brush and roller, QCF 341 Produce broken colour work and basic stenciling and QCF 342 Produce and apply complex stencil designs.

This unit also contains material that supports TAP Units Produce broken colour work and basic stencilling and Produce basic brush graining and marbling effects.

This unit will cover the following learning outcomes:

- Producing quality finish ground coats for painted decorative work
- Producing broken colour effects using water-based and solvent-based scumbles
- Preparing stencil plates from given design and applying stencils
- Producing wood and marble effects using basic techniques
- Producing basic textured finishes using brush and roller

Functional skills

When reading and understanding the text in this unit, you are practising several functional skills;

FE 1.2.1 – Identifying how the main points and ideas are organised in different texts

FE 1.2.2 – Understanding different texts in detail

FE 1.2.3 – Read different texts and take appropriate action, e.g. respond to advice/instructions

If there are any words or phrases that you do not understand, use a dictionary, look them up using the Internet or discuss with your tutor.

Did you know?

As the name suggests, specialist coatings are created to imitate natural products such as marbles and wood grains, so it is important that these effects look as natural as possible.

If the application method is incorrect, the finished effect will look artificial and therefore will not work.

K1. Producing quality finish ground coats for painted decorative work

When you are working to produce specialist decorative finishes, it is very important to have a good-quality finish on ground coats. Many of the skills you will need to produce high-quality base coats have been covered in earlier units. This section will briefly recap some of the key skills you will need to know.

Preparation processes for decorative work

Surfaces will need to be made good. Most surfaces need to be abraded to give a key for coatings to adhere to. You may also need to fill surfaces to remove dents, otherwise when the scumble is applied it will collect in them. It will show up as darker areas on the finished effect.

Defects that may occur as a result of low quality of ground coat finish

If the surfaces have not been prepared correctly prior to applying ground coats, there is a range of defects that could appear on your finished specialist decorative effect.

- **Bittiness** – occurs if you have not abraded correctly and or dusted off debris after rubbing down.
- **Ropiness** – occurs if the surface has not been given a full ground coat, making the finished specialist coating look thin and see-through.
- **Uneven colour** – occurs if indentations on the surface have not been filled correctly, meaning the finished coat will not spread out evenly.
- **Sinking** – occurs if spot priming has not been done correctly. The oil in the specialist coating evaporates too quickly if applied on top of a filler, making the coating appear uneven.

How application method may affect quality

It is important to apply the selected specialist coating correctly to avoid any defects occurring, such as brush marks, misses, runs, flashing and wet edges. These defects will affect the appearance of the work and mean the surface will lose the desired effect.

Benefits of using a stipple brush and roller

It is important to remove brush marks from your specialist effect so the desired effect will look as natural as possible. Using stipple brushes and rollers will eliminate these and ensure the ground coat has been applied evenly. This will aid with the application of the specialist coating.

Appropriate coating types for decorative work

When applying decorative specialist effects, the most appropriate coatings used for ground coats and base coats are neutral coloured vinyl silk emulsions and neutral coloured eggshell paints.

Usually the ground coat is a tone lighter than the lightest part of the desired finish, so using neutral colours as base coats will create the desired effect. These coatings are ideal as base coats and can be covered with the desired specialist paint effect colour. Both oil- and water-based paints can be used as ground coats, depending on which system you are using for your specialist decorative effect.

K2. Producing broken colour effects using water-based and solvent-based scumbles

In this section, we will look at some of the many special paint effects that can be created by a decorator. For broken colour effects you will need a clean and hard surface with no brush marks, indents or nibs. You will also need a good-quality base coat, such as an oil-based or water-based eggshell.

Materials used to produce broken colour effects

There are four common methods used to produce broken colour effects:

- rag rolling
- dragging
- glaze and wipe
- sponge stippling (additive and subtractive).

Scumble

Scumble is a base to which colour is added to create your specific effect. When you apply a scumble you are actually applying a thin film of colour (after adding colour to the scumble). This represents the finish you want to imitate for your specialist coating, for example, light oak. You will need to make sure that you have mixed it to the correct viscosity otherwise the finished effect will appear thin and colourless.

> **Remember**
>
> Overcoats can be opaque or translucent. A translucent coating means you can see through it, for example clear varnishes. Opaque coating means it will obliterate, or totally cover, a surface with the colour used.

> **Safety tip**
>
> Make sure you are wearing the correct PPE when producing special effects.

> **Key term**
>
> **Scumble** – a semi-transparent stain or glaze applied over a hard, dry ground coat

Did you know?

It is also possible to buy and use coloured glazes.

Key terms

Yellowing – is a defect caused by age and occurs when white oil-based coatings have been used on surfaces and the surface receives little natural light

Drier – a liquid chemical that promotes drying

A glaze is usually a clear coating applied to add shine and can change the colour cast or texture of the specialist surface you have created. It also helps to protect the finished surface. The main ingredients you will need to create an oil-based glaze are raw linseed oil, white spirit and liquid **driers**. You need to mix three parts white spirit, one part linseed oil and a small amount of drier (if mixing a litre of glaze, add a teaspoon amount of driers).

If you use oil-based coatings for decorative effects, **yellowing** will occur with age. This can be avoided with acrylic coatings, although these do not last as long as oil-based coatings. To help with the application of oil-based coatings, use white spirit to thin your coating out and add driers to speed up the drying process.

Mixing insufficient scumble

To create a uniform effect on a surface, you will need to mix enough scumble to paint the surface in one go. It will be impossible to mix a second identical batch of scumble, meaning the second mix will not be a uniform match for the first. Therefore it is worthwhile to mix slightly more scumble than you estimate you may need.

Drying times of scumbles

During the application of special effects you may need to reduce or extend the drying times of both oil-based and acrylic scumbles. There are several methods used to increase drying times.

Method	Description
Linseed oil	Used in oil-based scumbles to extend the working time so the effect can be created without drying and leaving an edge. Often used when applying the scumble over a large area.
Driers	Blends of chemicals added to paints to speed up drying time. Can be added to oil and alkyd paints and varnishes and to old coatings that have lost their usual drying times due to age.
Glycerine	Liquid (chemical material) diluted with water and added to acrylic paints to extend their working time. Allows the decorator to have more time to finish a task.
Lightspray	Used when delaying the drying process of a water-based scumble. Involves spraying water onto the effect, giving the painter more time to finish before drying.
Wet rag	When rag rolling, wet the rag to extend the working time of the scumble. If the rag is dry then scumble will be absorbed into the rag before it can be applied to the surface.

Table 22.1 Methods of increasing drying times of scumbles

Completing work

You need to complete the job in a single painting session. A delay in working – either due to taking a break, or stopping work over night – will allow part of the surface to dry before you have painted the rest. This difference will be clearly noticeable in the final job. If you are painting a large surface you must make sure that you have planned enough time to complete the work in one session.

If the surface is particularly large, it is best to have two or more operatives to complete the work; for example one operative can apply the scumble glaze and another operative can follow along, creating the effect to the applied glaze. This will help to keep continuity in the effect and will avoid introducing breaks in the effect.

Rag rolling

Rag rolling is a broken colour effect created by applying or lifting off colour with a rag or cloth. 'Ragging on' is the name given to the action of applying the colour to a ground coat. 'Ragging off' is the name given to the action of lifting off some of the colour and creates a different effect. The rag used should be a **lint**-free cloth and bunched up in the hand during paint application.

Chamois leather is often used to create the rag roll effect and is bunched together and rolled across the surface in different directions to give the effect. You can also use a chamois leather roller (Duet® type) or rolled-up paper or plastic bags instead of a rag to create softer or sharper effects.

Procedure for ragging on

- Mix up a coloured glaze, either an oil-based glaze or an acrylic glaze, and pour into a work pot. To create your specific coloured glaze, use either an oil colourant or an acrylic colourant and add it to (tint) your clear glaze.
- Bunch up a rag and dip it into the coloured glaze, making sure the rag is completely saturated.
- Wring out the rag and roll it into a loose cylinder, twisting it slightly.
- Apply the paint by rolling the rag across small sections of the surface in random directions to create a rag rolled finish. Overlap each section by a third to prevent stripes, banding or tracking occurring.

Remember

If you use water-based materials you will have to be aware that these dry more quickly than oil-based materials because of evaporation. When you are creating special effects using these paints, work in small manageable sections to keep the overall effect looking consistent.

Key term

Lint – tiny, fuzzy fibres of material

Safety tips

Remember to protect your hands by using a suitable barrier cream before carrying out the process.
Paint-soaked rags should be opened out and allowed to dry before disposal – wet rags are a fire risk due to spontaneous combustion, so never place them in your overall pockets!

Did you know?

A good method of applying this effect is to have one person applying the glaze and another person following along to create the desired effect.

Figure 22.1 A rag rolling paint effect can be more interesting than solid colour

Figure 22.2 A comb can be used to create a simple paint effect, as shown here, or more intricate patterns with practice

Procedure for ragging off

- Apply a coloured glaze to the surface, removing any brush marks with a hog hair stippler.
- Bunch up a rag and roll it across the surface in different directions. Move from top to bottom and make sure that you overlap by a third to prevent stripes or banding. This method will remove coloured glaze from the surface.
- Clean off the rag and repeat the process, remembering to alter the direction of the rag as it is rolling across the surface. This will prevent the finished effect from looking uniform.

Dragging and combing

Dragging and combing are decorative effects usually associated with graining, but are created with paint colours and glazes, rather than graining colours. When used with broken colour, dragging and combing produces a stylised version of the grain effect. An oil-based ground coat colour is best, but water based can be used. Dragging can be used on wall areas, window frames, door panels, etc. It is possible to produce many patterns by dragging and combing, including a straight timber grain, raw silk and even woven cotton combing effects.

Dragging

Step 1 Apply the glaze sparingly to the surface, laying off vertically

Step 2 Drag a brush through the glaze to create uneven lines. The ground coat should show through just enough to create a two-tone effect. Remember to keep the brush strokes parallel and straight, remove any build up of glaze from the brush with a clean cloth to prevent the effect being spoiled.

Texture designs for ceilings and walls

Stipple, bark and swirl effects are commonly used when applying textured finishes.

- A stipple effect is mainly used on ceilings as it is a basic and easy pattern to achieve and is used to hide indentations on ceilings.

- The swirl effect is also used on ceilings and is created by turning the stipple brush in circles when it is against the textured finish.

- A bark effect is usually used on walls to create a wood effect design and is created using a special bark roller, rolled onto the textured paint in straight lines representing wood grain (see pages 216–17).

Figure 22.24 Stipple effect

Figure 22.25 Bark effect

Using ready-mixed and self-mixed paints

The advantage of a ready-mixed texture material is that you can start to apply it as soon as you want without mixing time. It is also consistent in colour, viscosity and working time. The main disadvantage of using a ready-mixed texture material will be cost, as it is only sold in containers ranging from 2.5 to 5 litres. It is also only available in predetermined consistencies which could restrict the number of patterns you can apply.

If mixing your own paint, it is important to mix the correct consistency of textured paint. Some patterns will need a heavy textured effect, such as broken leather. Other patterns, like a stipple effect, can be applied thickly or thinly depending on what the client wants.

Sand type paint comes ready-made, but you can create it yourself by mixing the colour and type of paint with sand or grit. This type of textured paint is usually used to create a non-slip floor paint. Plaster of Paris type paint also comes ready-made, and again you can create it yourself, this time by mixing the powder with clean water. Take care when mixing either of these types of textured paint yourself, as you can easily create a cloud of powder or sand: make sure you are wearing a suitable dust mask.

Plaster of Paris type

With the plaster of Paris type, you apply the mixture (powder and water mixed) to the surface with a brush or roller, then use a variety of tools to create the different finishes and patterns required:

- **stipple brush** – for swirls, stipple, broken swirl and broken leather
- **texturing combs** – for circles, fans, baskets and combinations of circle with fan, etc. Texturing combs also work well for producing patterns around light fittings, and can create decorative borders
- **pattern roller** – for bark and other wood effects
- **lacing tool** – to smooth the tips of denser, abstract wall texture patterns such as bark, swirl and broken leather. This tool is a blade that can remove high build-up of spikes, etc. created with the patterns above, making textures on walls and ceilings safer.

If you ever need to remove a textured pattern from a surface when decorating, you must:

- scrape the entire surface with a suitable scraper
- soak warm water into the texture with a sponge until you have saturated it
- carry on scraping until you get to the bottom surface.

Sand type

The second type of textured paint (sand added to water-based/oil-based paint) can also be applied to surfaces with either a brush or roller, although you will not normally create any patterns with this type of textured paint.

Purpose and timing for finishing processes

It is important to create a margin around your final design to make your finished job look more professional. This margin will act as a border around features, such as light fittings, switches and the outside edges of surfaces. It must be done when the paint is wet, before it hardens and becomes unworkable.

It is a good idea to do an example piece first, to make sure that the client is happy with the finish. Some patterns, such as stipple effects, have heavy looking textures and you may have to remove the tips with a lacing tool to avoid any hazards.

To achieve this, hold the lacing tool (usually triangular in shape) at an angle and lightly smooth the textured paint as it starts to firm up. Keep the lacer damp by wetting as, if it is left to dry, it will begin to drag the textured paint and damage the overall look.

Lacing will level and flatten most textured finishes and remove high points and build up. If these are not laced when the paint is wet, you will need to remove them at a later point which will cause damage to the finished effect.

Figure 22.26 Lacing

Did you know?

When applying texture paint in high temperatures it may start to set sooner than normal. It is best to apply paint to small manageable areas and create your chosen pattern straight away, keeping a wet edge going throughout the process. In incorrect temperatures the paint could dry almost immediately, causing defects or leading to the paint dropping or losing definition.

FAQ

How many operatives would be needed to complete a rag rolled effect to a large wall or ceiling area?

Due to the application system of creating a rag rolled special effect, three operatives would be the ideal number to have to complete the task: one person to apply the glaze, followed by the second person stippling out the brush marks and finally the third person carrying out the task of rag rolling, all of which would ensure that the task is completed with the minimum of fuss and thus avoiding defects.

What does the term 'broken colour' mean?

A 'broken colour' paint effect is one that is created by layering paint colours and then breaking them up to reveal the underlying colours. This can be achieved by adding colour (for example, when sponging) or by taking off colour (for example, when ragging off). A broken colour effect can give a surface the appearance of shade and texture.

Check it out

1 Describe some of the defects that can occur from a low quality of ground coat finish.

2 Prepare a method statement explaining the process used to mix and calculate quantities of scumbles and glazes for a range of different colours and surfaces.

3 Describe the process used for rag rolling and state which two types of material could be used instead of a rag to lift off colour.

4 Explain the types of pattern that can be achieved by dragging and combing.

5 State the purpose of sponging and stippling and explain the effects that can be created by this process.

6 Explain what a relief surface is and state how it affects decisions about decoration.

7 Explain two methods used to create stencils, and describe the methods used to treat stencil plates.

8 Prepare a method statement explaining the planning that is required when applying stencils to a range of four different surfaces. Use sketches and diagrams to illustrate this statement.

9 Explain how to enlarge and reduce the design of a stencil and why this might be necessary when working.

10 Describe the ingredients used for creating a water-graining medium and for marble effects. Explain how this is mixed in order to create the required coating.

11 Using sketches and diagrams explain the processes used to create a marbling and a graining effect.

12 Explain why a client might wish to use textured paint and explain the surfaces that should be used and the advantages and disadvantages of using ready-mixed and self-mixed paints.

Getting ready for assessment

The information contained in this unit, as well as continued practical assignments that you will carry out in your college or training centre, will help you in preparing for both your end-of-unit test and the diploma multiple-choice test. It will also aid you in preparing for the work that is required for the synoptic practical assignments.

Many of the decorating jobs you carry out will require a special finish made to a surface, either to create an effect or to imitate another type of surface, such as wood or marble. In these cases, it is essential to have a clear idea from the client of the work they wish to have done. You will also need to make sure that you have prepared all surfaces correctly – as this is to be the key decorative effect for the surface, it is vital that it is free from defects. You will need to know the basic skills for creating a range of decorative effects, and be confident in using these methods.

You will need to be familiar with:

* producing high-quality finish ground coats for painted decorative work
* producing broken colour effects using water-based and solvent-based scumbles
* preparing stencil plates from given designs and applying stencils
* producing wood and marble effects using basic techniques
* producing basic textured finishes using brush and roller.

For learning outcome four you will need to be able to check factors related to the suitability of a ground coat and rectify any defects you may discover. You will need to be able to select the correct colourants and pigments, appropriate to the wood or marble effect you wish to create. You will then need to prepare these materials for application in the correct way, mixing glazes and ensuring that you have the correct tools and equipment. You will need to follow the correct practical methods to create the effects, working to current environmental and relevant health and safety legislation. At the end of your work you will need to be able to clean and maintain tools, brushes and equipment before storing them away.

Before you carry out any work, you should outline a plan of action, which will give you the order you need to do things in. It will also record a rough timescale for the work you need to carry out, in order to make sure that you complete everything you need to do safely. You will need to refer back to this plan at each stage, to make sure that you are not making any mistakes as you work. This is particularly important when applying decorative paint effects as these are intended to be the 'showpiece' of the final job. If you do not plan correctly when working on these, you will reduce the final quality of the job and this will reflect badly on your own skills.

Your speed in carrying out any tasks in a practice setting will also help to prepare you for the time set for the test. However, you must never rush the test! Always make sure you are working safely. Make sure throughout the test that you are wearing the appropriate PPE and using tools correctly.

Good luck!

CHECK YOUR KNOWLEDGE

1 If the surface you plan to apply decorative effects to has not been prepared correctly what defect will occur?

 a bittiness

 b ropiness

 c uneven colour

 d all of the above

2 Why are stipple brushes and rollers used to create specialist effects?

 a to remove brush marks

 b to soften colours

 c to apply the effect

 d none of the above

3 What coatings are best used for ground coats when producing specialist effects?

 a clear oil-based varnish

 b dark coloured gloss

 c neutral coloured eggshell/emulsion

 d coloured oil-based varnish

4 Which method is ideal for creating broken colour effects?

 a rag rolling

 b stencilling

 c texturing

 d graining

5 How can you protect decorative effects?

 a apply a transparent glaze

 b apply an opaque glaze

 c apply a preservative

 d apply a stain

6 How do you protect your hands when applying specialist effects?

 a use thick rubber gloves

 b use a barrier cream

 c use hot soapy water before applying

 d use fuller's earth

7 Which BS 4800 number represents the colour used for a ground coat when creating a pine effect?

 a 06C33

 b 08C35

 c 04D44

 d 04D46

8 When creating a stencil, how can you protect it from damage?

 a keep it clean

 b coat it in shellac or linseed oil

 c use low tack masking tape

 d all of the above

9 Which textured paint effect is best suited to walls rather than ceilings?

 a stipple effect

 b swirl effect

 c bark effect

 d fan effect

10 Which tool is used to remove peaks and sharp tips from textured paint effects?

 a stipple brush

 b dusting brush

 c scraper

 d lacing tool

UNIT 2023

Know how to apply water-based paint systems using high volume low pressure (HVLP) spray equipment

High Volume Low Pressure (HVLP) spraying is a technological solution for applying large amounts of paint or coatings to surfaces. This method is far more efficient than other methods; it means you can spray large areas with the same colour or spray intricate surfaces such as mouldings and fancy plasterwork, with a lot less fuss. As a painter and decorator, you may need to use spray equipment at some point in your career.

This unit contains material that supports NVQ unit QCF 340 Apply coatings by the air spray method.

This unit also contains material that supports TAP Units Apply coatings by the airless spray method and Apply coatings by the air spray method.

In this unit we will cover the following learning outcomes:

■ Preparing work areas by protecting surrounding areas, furniture and fittings
■ Setting up HVLP spray equipment and preparing materials for spray application
■ Applying water-based coatings by HVLP spray
■ Rectifying faults in spray equipment and defects in applied coatings
■ Cleaning, maintaining and storing HVLP spray equipment and materials.

Unit 2023 Know how to apply water-based paint systems using HVLP spray equipment

K1. Preparing work areas by protecting surrounding areas, furniture and fittings

Site preparation is important for all painters and decorators but especially when applying coatings to surfaces by spray painting. Surface preparation was covered earlier in Unit 2020, pages 134–36. This section will give more information on protective sheeting and masking tape.

Speed and quality of finish are the main advantages of paint spraying, but one of the major disadvantages of this method is overspray. The HVLP system reduces this problem, but does not remove it. Overspray occurs because you cannot cut in effectively with a spray gun: there is always a degree of 'bounce back' of paint from the surface being sprayed.

Spraying interiors

If you had to spray the interior of a commercial building, such as an office, you would first need to mask any windows so that the paint could not damage them. To do this, you would cover the glass with a masking paper and masking tape, making sure that the paper was overlapped correctly and sealed with tape.

If you were spraying the interior of a house, and only the walls and ceiling were to be sprayed, you would first have to make sure that all removable items were taken out, then mask up any items that could not be removed (carpets, skirting boards, etc.). Carpets must be protected with dust sheets, covered with polythene sheeting and then taped up correctly around the room; skirting boards and architrave around doors would need taping up with a low-tack masking tape, applied correctly with no gaps.

Buildings such as factories also need the correct masking, as there could be expensive items, for example machinery or tiled floors, that need protecting. You would have to mask correctly any pipes, electric cables and tubing that were not being sprayed, using polythene sheets and masking tape, ensuring there were no gaps or spaces. To protect the flooring, you would use sheets of hardboard, corrugated plastic or heavy cardboard, sealed around the floor edges with a heavy, well-applied masking tape. As the sprayer would be walking around the area, the masking would need to be sturdy enough not to lift, letting overspray hit the floor.

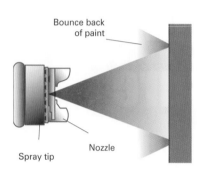

Figure 23.1 Bounce back of paint when spraying

Bounce back of paint

Spray tip

Nozzle

When you have checked all the equipment thoroughly, and you have all the necessary PPE/RPE on, you are then ready to start your spraying job.

Gravity, suction and pressure feed spray guns

Spray guns are designed to atomise fluids at the tip of the nozzle to make application easier. Gravity feed and suction feed spray guns have two passageways fixed at the nozzle, one for the fluid and one for the air. Atomisation is achieved by a vacuum formed by the rush of air moving past the fluid passage while drawing fluid into the air stream. At this point of contact the fluid is mixed with air and a spray mist leaves the nozzle under pressure.

Figure 23.10 An air compressor

Gravity feed

A gravity feed gun has a container fixed to the top of the gun. The coating is fed into the gun by the coating pressing down towards the nozzle of the gun. Because the coating is gravity fed, less air pressure is required to atomise the coating. This creates less overspray and therefore less waste. Gravity feed guns are therefore ideal for details and spot repairs.

> **Remember**
>
> Suction feed guns are better suited when changing colours regularly and when small tasks are required, such as touch ups.

Suction feed

A suction feed gun has a container fixed to the bottom of the gun and draws the fluid to the gun by suction. This requires more air pressure than the gravity feed system in order to create a strong enough vacuum to pull the coating up the feeding tube from the container. It creates more overspray. It is possible to atomise at a lower air pressure by pressurising the cup, forcing the fluid up the feed tube. The cup can be pressurised by an air tube extending from the air supply to the cup.

Pressure feed

A pressure feed gun operates by positive pressure. This means the air is fed to the container causing a pressure vacuum. This system sends the fluid and air directly to the gun. The coating container is usually kept some distance from the spray gun to aid application. It requires long **air** and **fluid lines**. It is normally used for large areas where a faster application is required and for heavier coatings.

> **Key terms**
>
> **Air line** – used during spraying to transport the air. A high volume air line is used with HVLP spray equipment to operate the gun when the coating is being atomised
>
> **Fluid line** – used to transport the coating to the gun during spraying

Figure 23.11 Air spray gun

Types of spray gun

Air spray (conventional)

Paint is applied to the part by pneumatic fluid atomisation at higher air pressures. Air spray guns come in a variety of configurations: siphon feed, gravity feed, and pressure feed. This type of spray gun is most commonly used for industrial finishing.

- **Advantages** – complete pattern control. Finest atomisation. Good for high-production rate applications.
- **Limitations** – uses more air. Creates the most fog. Low transfer efficiency.

HVLP

This is similar to the air spray gun in that it uses pneumatic fluid atomisation, except that HVLP uses a higher volume of air at a lower pressure. The lower pneumatic pressure allows for less overspray. HVLP spray guns come in a variety of styles: siphon feed, gravity feed and pressure feed.

- **Advantages** – high transfer efficiency (65 per cent to 75 per cent). Sprays well into recesses and cavities.
- **Limitations** – uses a high volume of air. Atomisation not as fine as air spray guns.

Airless and air-assisted airless

Here atomisation is caused by the release of high-pressure fluid through a small opening. Airless atomisation can be assisted by air atomisation (air-assisted airless) to provide a finer finish and break up the tailing effect at the edge of the spray pattern. This method is most widely used by painting contractors, structural metal finishers and heavy equipment manufacturers.

- **Advantages** – high fluid capability. Large patterns. Fastest spray application process. Low air consumption. Limited fog and bounce back – permits spraying into cavities.
- **Limitations** – potentially hazardous hydraulic injection. Higher rate of overspray due to high fluid output. Sharp patterns: difficult to blend. Expensive nozzles (tips). Coarse atomisation may flood surface or create runs. Equipment requires high levels of maintenance.

Electrostatic

Electrostatic spray guns are usually used in spray painting factories or booths. With these guns, the material is atomised in the same way as conventional air (pneumatic), airless (fluid impingement), air-assisted airless or rotary guns.

The difference is the way in which the paint is attracted to the surface. The particles of paint become electrically charged and are attracted to the surface to be painted, which has the opposite charge. The electricity may be turned off to permit normal spraying.

- **Advantages** – a 'wrap around' effect: you can coat the back of the part while spraying from the front for example, you can coat both sides of a wire mesh fence by spraying from the front. Minimised overspray means material savings. Can be used with or without electrical charge.
- **Limitations** – some conductive materials require special equipment or paint reformulation. Parts must be conductive and have capacity to be grounded. Difficult to penetrate cavities or recesses with power supply on.

Spray gun components

There are several components you will need to be familiar with when working with spray guns. These are covered in Table 23.01. Gun set-up is the term used to describe all the components of the gun when it has been assembled together.

> **Did you know?**
>
> Many household items, such as washing machines, are painted using electrostatic spray painting. Each item is painted, then put in an oven to 'set' the paint.

Component	Function
Spray gun body	The actual main component, it allows the user to apply coatings to the surfaces. All the other components are attached to it
Air inlet connector	Where the air hose connects to the gun, enabling it to spray the coating
Air valve	Allows the user to adjust the flow of air to the gun during spray application
Trigger	When pulled by the user, allows the coating to be sprayed to the surface from the gun
Air cap	There are different types of air caps used with spraying systems: • External caps mix and atomise air and fluid outside the air cap. Good for applying all types of coatings, especially fast-drying coatings and high-quality finishes • Internal caps mix air and fluid inside the cap before expelling them. Used where low pressures and small volumes of coatings are required. Rarely used for finishing when fast drying coatings are being sprayed or for high quality finishes All air caps must match the baffles used on the guns otherwise failure and faults may occur
Fluid needle	Where the coating passes through the gun and opens/closes the fuel passages
Fluid tip	Where the fluid needle is seated in the nozzle of the gun
Air baffle	Forms part of the air cap and fluid tip, holding the fluid tip in place and forming a positive air seal to prevent faults and loss of air
Fluid needle packing	Forms a seal on the needle to prevent fluid leaking from the gun unnecessarily when the trigger is not being pulled. It is also adjustable to allow coatings through the needle when spraying.
Spreader control valve	Adjusts the size of the spray pattern when spraying fluids onto surfaces
Fluid needle adjuster	Controls the flow of the fluid from the gun and allows accurate adjustments, helping the needle with wear and tear

Table 23.1 Spray gun components

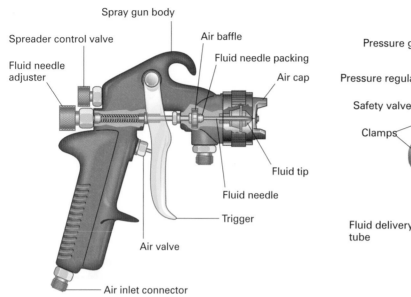

Figure 23.12 Spray gun components

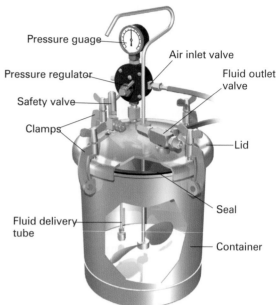

Figure 23.13 Pressure pot components

Pressure pot components

Pressure feed tanks and pots are used when large quantities of paint or coatings are to be sprayed.

Component	Function
Container	Main body of the equipment containing the coating to be sprayed, used with pressure feed systems
Lid	Top of the container, which must be sealed shut during use
Clamps	Used to keep the lid sealed while being used
Seal	Positioned between lid and container to keep the equipment together during use
Air inlet valve	Where air hose attached to equipment during use
Pressure regulator	Allows the user to either turn the pressure up or down depending on level needed to spray coating correctly
Pressure gauge	Allows the user to see how much pressure is present in the container at time of application
Safety valve	For releasing any build up of pressure in the system
Fluid delivery tube	Where the coating flows through the machine during application
Fluid outlet valve	Fluid lines attachment so application of coatings can happen

Table 23.2 Pressure pot components

Other components used for spray painting

There is a wide range of other components and tools that you may encounter while working with HVLP equipment.

Component	Function
Turbine unit	The power supply for the spray unit used during spraying
Compressor	Available in petrol, diesel and electric models. Used to power spray equipment and other items used
Transformer	Used on site to allow power tools to operate (110 volts), even when the main voltage is a domestic voltage (230 volts)
Extension cable	Used in conjunction with a transformer, allows you to use power tools without being right next to the power source

Table 23.3 Other components for spray painting

Assembly sequence for component parts and spray systems

The correct sequence of assembling the HVLP equipment is as follows.

Step 1 Select all relevant equipment needed for your system

- extension cable
- turbine unit
- HV (high volume) air line
- the selected gun can be either a gravity or suction feed gun.

Step 2 Fix the extension cable to your turbine unit so it can be kept away from the area being sprayed.

Step 3 To prevent any damage from overspray, choose the correct needle for the gun, then fix the HV air line to spray gun.

Step 4 After mixing the coating pour the correct amount into the gun's container, turn on the turbine, test the spray gun and selected spray fan. You are now ready to apply the coating to the surface.

Figure 23.14 Transformer

Figure 23.15 Compressor

Pressure feed systems

There is a different process for pressure feed systems.

Step 1 Select the correct ACO (air compression outfit) for the job and connect it to a transformer to use 110 V equipment.

Step 2 Select the pressure feed gun and the correct needle set up for the task.

Step 3 Select the correct size pressure pot for the job.

Step 4 Attach the air line from the compressor to the gun and pressure pot.

Step 5 Connect the fluid line to the pressure pot and spray gun.

Step 6 Mix the correct amount of fluid, strain and then pour into the pressure pot.

Step 7 Seal the pressure pot and lid using clamps on pot.

Step 8 When all of the equipment is connected, do a test with the spray gun to adjust spray fan and then carry out spraying task.

Adjustments to ensure correct spraying/application

When using spray equipment, always make sure you have selected the correct needle set-up and that air is flowing through the gun. You must make sure the spray fan is the correct size for the job.

After testing the equipment works, carry out a spray test by pulling the trigger of the gun and spraying paint onto a test area. Using the pattern control knob, adjust the size of the fan pattern to the desired size for the application of coatings to the surface.

Air pressure and equipment checks

Once you have selected the correct spray painting equipment and necessary PPE and RPE (see below for more on RPE), you need to check all components before you use them. This will prevent possible accidents to yourself and others, and will avoid problems with the job at hand.

You will need to check that there is an air supply to the spray gun, by checking the compressor/generator that supplies the air. The air is supplied to the gun via a hose, and within this air stream there is a region of low pressure. Check the hose for any damage, as this could cause a lack of pressure, causing problems when you apply the paint.

The gun has a trigger mechanism, which opens and closes a nozzle mounted in the gun. Around the nozzle, there are lots of holes through which air is expelled. You need to check both the nozzle and the trigger for any blockages or old paint/debris as this will also cause production problems.

Health and safety when spraying

For many of the details of health and safety when spraying, you will need to refer back to Unit 1001 page 25 for details of PPE, eye irritation and ingestion, COSHH regulations and the Health and Safety at Work Act. In this section we will look at some specific issues related to HVLP spray equipment.

As a paint sprayer working in the painting and decorating industry, you face many dangers; but your training will help you to protect yourself from hazards. If you do not protect yourself, and you are involved in an accident, you will suffer immediate injury. Paint sprayers often face less obvious, more **insidious** hazards than conventional painters, which can result in death. These hazards are not always recognised until it is too late, so make sure you read the following section carefully.

Using the correct protection

The main hazard you will face as a paint sprayer comes from the fumes and mists given off during the application of paints and coatings. As well as the PPE you need to wear for all tasks as a painter and decorator, you will need to use RPE (respiratory protective equipment). RPE includes a variety of different spray masks.

- **Filter respirator** – this is fitted with one or two disposable cartridge filters. It is important to select the correct type of filter to suit the nature of the hazard, and to replace filters as necessary. As with all masks, there are advantages and disadvantages with this type of mask (see Table 23.4).
- **Air-fed respirator** – this is made up of a full head set and regulator worn by the sprayer, which is connected to an air filtration unit. The filtration unit converts compressed air into clean, breathable air. The compressor must be situated well away from the work area.
- **Powered respirator** – this has a battery-operated motor, which supplies the head set with filtered air. There are two types of powered respirator: one has a separate motor and filter away from the headset; the other has these items integrated into the helmet.

Remember

If you clean and maintain your equipment correctly, you should not encounter any problems with blockages or old paint and debris.

Key term

Insidious – advancing without you realising it; treacherous

Unit 2023

Know how to apply water-based paint systems using HVLP spray equipment

Mask type	Advantages	Disadvantages
Filter respirator	• Cartridge filters can be selected to offer protection against toxic vapours and dust • Suitable when spraying some solvent-based coatings in well-ventilated areas • Can be worn with safety goggles	• Expensive compared to dust masks • Can become uncomfortable when worn for long periods • Not suitable for use in oxygen-deficient areas • Not suitable for use in confined spaces • Cartridge filters have a limited life and must be replaced regularly • Require hygienic maintenance (regular cleaning)
Air-fed respirator	• Effective against the most toxic carcinogenic/isocyanate two-pack paint coatings • Offers eye and respiratory protection • Protects against toxic dusts, gases and vapours • Particularly useful in confined spaces • Offers all-round vision	• Expensive to buy and maintain • Needs special training • Can be cumbersome and uncomfortable over long periods • Visors can be coated with spray mist • Needs a suitable compressor
Powered respirator	• Offers head, eye and respiratory protection • Protects against toxic dusts, gases and vapours • Particularly useful on demolition and refurbishment work • Offers all-round vision	• Expensive to buy and maintain (batteries, filters and visors) • Can be cumbersome and uncomfortable over long periods • Visors can be coated with spray mist

Table 23.4 RPE spray masks

K3. Applying water-based coatings by HVLP spray

Many coatings and paints can be applied by brush and roller, but only those mentioned below can be sprayed onto a surface – again, provided you have prepared the paint and surface correctly.

Water-based coatings that can be used in spraying

- acrylic primer/undercoat
- matt emulsion paints
- vinyl silk emulsion paints
- masonry paints (water based)
- moisture vapour permeable coating
- low-odour eggshell finish
- emulsion varnish
- wood stain
- quick-drying acrylic metal primer
- blockfiller

Solvent-based coatings that can be used in spraying

- alkali-resisting primer
- etch primer
- zinc chromate metal primer
- zinc-rich epoxy primer
- eggshell/satin finish
- multicolour finish (fleck)
- masonry paint (oil-based)
- cellulose coating
- moisture vapour permeable/microporous coatings (spirit-based)

- anti-graffiti paint
- chlorinated rubber paint
- machinery enamel
- epoxy resin paint
- flame retardant paint
- micaceous iron oxide paint
- oil-based wood stain
- oil resin varnishes
- interior varnishes

Importance of viscosity and using strained paint

Before any spraying can be carried out you must make sure that the paint is at the right **viscosity**: if it is not, you will not be able to apply the paint or coating to the surface you are supposed to be painting. Follow the manufacturer's instructions and you will mix the required coating to the right consistency for spraying. Thorough, detailed and well-written instructions (especially with regard to thinning) are crucial for maximising performance. Everything that goes through an HVLP sprayer must be thinned properly. If you do not follow the instructions carefully, you leave everything to chance. The result could be the paint or coating not spraying correctly, the gun clogging up and not working, or producing a substandard finish to the job.

Measuring viscosity

When spraying any coating, the manufacturer recommends the correct flow rate needed for spraying. A viscometer is used to achieve this measurement. After mixing the coating with a thinner, pour the coating into the viscosity cup (the ford cup). The fluid will drain through a small hole at the bottom of the cup and, while this is happening, time the flow of the fluid leaving the cup.

Mixing ratios can be stated either in parts or percentages. Parts (normally by volume) are the most commonly used method and the easiest to understand. When a mixing ratio is given in parts, the measurement chosen as one part can vary due to the device you are using to measure. Regardless of the size, the chosen measurement device must be used throughout the mixing process.

Remember

When mixing fluids for spraying you need to know how much thinner is needed to be added to the coating (base coat); you may even need to know how to mix a two-pack coating in the same way.

Key term

Viscosity – the thickness of a liquid

Figure 23.16 Viscometer

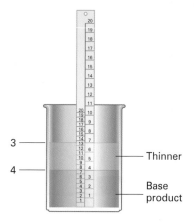

Figure 23.17 Using a ratio stick

Functional skills

When working out amounts for mixing, you will be practising **FM 1.1.1** – which relates to identifying and selecting mathematical procedures. **FM 1.2.1a** – relates to using appropriate procedures, and this will be essential when calculating paint ratios.

Remember

Paint is heavier than solvent, which is why you always pour the heaviest product in to the container first to correctly measure out what is needed.

A mixing ratio given as 2:1 normally means it requires two parts base product (coating) and one part thinner. Another ratio often used for two pack coatings is 4:2:1, meaning four parts base product, two parts thinner and one part hardener.

Sometimes mixing ratios are given as percentages so you will need to convert the percentages to fractions. Think of the fractions as detailed below:

- 25% as a fraction would be ¼ = 1 part thinner, 4 parts paint
- 50% as a fraction would be ½ =1 part thinner, 2 parts paint
- 75% as a fraction would be ¾ = 3 parts thinner, 4 parts paint
- 100% as a fraction would be $^1/_1$ = 1 part thinner, 1 part paint.

Ratio sticks

A ratio stick has numbers equally spaced apart printed on it to check the amount of fluids added to a container, so measuring can be carried out. Use a flat bottomed container with parallel sides and hold the ratio stick vertically in the bottom. Pour your base product into the container, followed by the thinner. If you were using a mixing ratio of 4:3, you would first pour the base product into the container up to the number 4 on the ratio stick followed by adding the thinner up to the number 7. Then mix the two together, giving you the required amount.

Keeping paint clean

Another important point to keep in mind is to make sure that, after you have correctly mixed the paint or coating, you keep dirt and debris out of it. Small pieces of dirt or splinters of wood can easily become lodged in the tip of the gun, stopping it from spraying; dust stirred up by other trades could contaminate the paint and make it unusable. To prevent this from happening, use a paint strainer. This piece of equipment allows you to strain a good quantity of the paint into a clean, dust-free container.

WFT and DFT

WFT and DFT stand for Wet Film Thickness and Dry Film Thickness and are terms used when measuring thicknesses of coatings. When coatings have been sprayed on to the surfaces a measurement will be taken during its wet stage to check that the thickness of the coating is at the recommended level. Each coating needs to be measured during the process so the correct amount is applied in total.

The wet measurement will be taken with a wet film thickness gauge. This measures the thickness of the coating using **microns**. This is essential to ensure the correct dry film is present at the end of painting. When the coating is applied, the solvent starts to evaporate, meaning the WFT measurements are checked throughout application.

When the application process is finished the dry film thickness is also measured and, if any discrepancies are present in the thickness, then another application of paint can be added.

Effects of temperature, humidity and ventilation on viscosity and drying

We covered the effects of these factors on drying times earlier in Unit 2020, pages 149–50. Make sure that you have the correct atmospheric conditions while spraying coatings to prevent defects from occurring.

The spraying action

You must make sure you get the correct training before you try to complete a spraying task. Once trained, you should always follow these simple rules to achieve a perfect finish.

- Keep the distance between the gun and the surface as close as possible to the manufacturer's recommendation at all times.
- Move the spray gun parallel to the work, keeping the gun at a right angle.
- **Overlap** each successive stroke by 50 per cent.
- Trigger the spray gun at the beginning and end of each stroke, making sure that the gun is in motion before triggering. This will reduce overspray and runs.
- Optimise the fan size to suit the job/surface you are spraying.

It is important to keep the correct distance between the spray gun and the surface to be painted. If you place the gun too close to the surface, bounce back increases – resulting in poor finish quality: the paint or coating could run and sag. If you have too much distance between the gun and the surface, it can result in overshoot and 'paint fog' – where not enough paint/coating hits the surface, creating more overspray.

When first spraying, many people arc the spray gun automatically. You should not let this action develop into a habit, as **arcing** the gun results in an uneven finish: the coating will be the right thickness in the middle of a stroke but starved of coating at the edges.

Key term

Micron – one millionth of a metre

Remember

Litres per minute refers to how much coating you can spray during application.

Key terms

Overlap – this is where you apply coatings to a surface and then overlap each pass so the coating will become uniform on the surface (similar to when you are using a roller)

Arcing – creating an arc, or a section of a circle; when spraying a surface, this is when you curve your wrist, and the gun, resulting in an uneven finish to the paint/coating

Did you know?

Steel surfaces such as ships hulls, bridges and metal structures are usually spray painted. However domestic properties and factories also now have coatings applied to them in this way.

Unit 2023

Tilting the spray gun causes similar faults to arcing – excessive overspray and an uneven or patchy finish.

Always hold the gun perpendicular, or square to the surface. The correct spraying speed allows a full wet coat of paint or coating to be applied to the surface without any defects. You should move the gun in a confident, flowing fashion, without hesitation.

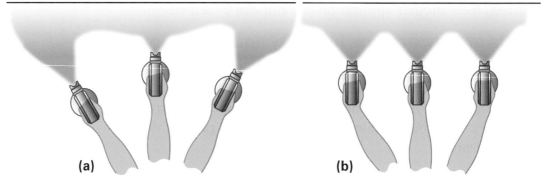

(a)   **(b)**

Figure 23.18 Incorrect (a) and correct (b) ways to hold the gun

Application techniques for obstacles

When carrying out spray painting jobs you may come across obstacles such as pipe work and fixed machinery, which cannot be removed. You will also need to spray surfaces with internal and external corners.

To make sure that the surfaces are coated correctly you may need to use paint brushes to help with the application, because of the awkwardness of these surfaces and to prevent overcoating. This is known as stripe coating, where internal corners and around pipe work, beams and machinery are painted in with a brush to avoid a build-up of paint, which could lead to runs and sagging. Some external corners may also need strip coating.

K4. Rectifying faults in spray equipment and defects in applied coatings

During spray painting you may come across several faults with the equipment. If you encounter these faults you need to be able to rectify them to complete your work.

Fault	Description of fault	Rectifying the fault
Electrical failure	No power feeds the machine	Must be rectified by a qualified electrician and the machine put in quarantine with a notice placed on it until it is fit for use
Dirty air cap	Causes faulty spray patterns	Remove and clean air cap with a suitable thinner or solvent, then replace
Dry needle packing	Causes fluid to leak or drip from the gun	Lubricate needle packing with mineral oil. Check packing nut as this may be too tight and need adjusting
Loose, damaged or worn fluid tip/needle	Causes leaking or dripping from the gun. Leads to runs and sags in coating and prevents gun from spraying correctly damaging spray patterns	Tighten fluid tip or needle and replace if worn or damaged
Incorrect set-up of fluid tip	Causes surface defects to applied coatings and leaking fluid	Remove the cap and top and correctly match up the items
Fluttering	Coating flutters, or spits, out of gun during application. Caused by obstruction in fluid passage or not enough fluid in container	Stop operation and remove obstruction then clean passage with solvent. Refill container and hold gun upright to avoid tipping the container. Check fluid tube or inlet nipple is tight
Defective spray patterns	Prevents coatings from assuming the correct pattern	Remove dirty cap or tip and any obstructions in air cap. Thoroughly clean items before resuming
Fluid leakage	Caused by missing or broken fluid needle spring	Replace damaged component. Check needle size is correct and is free from dirt
Kinked hoses	Causes system to lose pressure, leading to spray pattern problems	Fully unwind all hoses and allow them a clear space
Spluttering	Coating has trouble being released from the gun tip smoothly	Clean gun and check pressure is set correctly

Table 23.5 Defects when working with HLVP equipment

Material faults of contamination and incorrect viscosity

When applying coatings, it is important that you thin and strain your coating and that you have the correct viscosity. Common faults which will occur if you do not strain the coating include spluttering, blocked air holes and defective spray patterns. These could be caused by dirt or grit in the coating. Paint with an incorrect viscosity may not spray from the gun or clog the needle and tip. Paint which is too thin will leave the gun as a dry spray and evaporate.

Find out

Using manufacturer's advice and the Internet, find out what common thicknesses are recommended for spray painting.

> **Did you know?**
>
> Sags are similar to runs but caused when only a little too much coating has been applied. The same process should be used to rectify them.

Defects in applied coatings

The following defects can occur when you are applying coatings to surfaces using spray painting equipment.

- **Runs** – occur when too much coating has been applied to a surface and the paint runs straight away due to its thickness and weight. To rectify this, remove all excess coating and leave to dry then prepare the surface again, and reapply the coating.

- **Dry spray (overspray)** – occurs when the coating has lost too much solvent in the air before it reaches the surface, or the gun tip is too far away from the surface. In both cases only a thin amount of coating is visible on the surface. To rectify this make sure that you are at the correct distance from the surface before applying coatings.

- **Banding** – occurs when the coating has not been blended together during passes of the gun and shows on the surface in 'bands'. To rectify this make sure each pass during application overlaps the previous pass by at least 50 per cent.

- **Orange peel** – occurs when either too much or too little air pressure has been used during application. It resembles the skin of an orange on the surface of the coating after it has been sprayed. It can also be caused by the viscosity of the coating being too high or if incorrect thinners have been used. To rectify, prepare the surface again and use the correct pressure and thickness of coating.

K5. Cleaning, maintaining and storing HVLP spray equipment and materials

Using HVLP spray equipment can be dangerous. You will need to follow all safety advice and manufacturer's instructions to be sure you are working safely. Look back at Unit 1001 for more advice on working safely with electricity. When shutting down, turn off the power and release any pressure build up in the gun by pulling the trigger as you would when operating the system. By releasing this pressure you will avoid any accidents when dismantling the gun for cleaning. Always point the gun downwards, preferably into a large container, to release any pressure.

Cleaning HVLP equipment

It is easiest to clean away the coatings that you have used immediately after application, while the coating is still wet. At this point, you can flush away any unwanted material from the equipment with water or solvent – which is nearly impossible to do if you let the coating dry in the spray equipment.

You should clean your spray equipment as follows:

- When the job has been completed, empty any remaining paint/coating back into your main pot, making sure you have removed all traces of the coating from your spray container.

- Depending on which model of HVLP system you have used, spray or run a quantity of clean water or solvent through the system, until it is perfectly clear. If it is not, dried coatings can build up in the lines, possibly breaking away, contaminating fresh coatings and blocking the nozzle.

- Fill the container with clean thinners, and reconnect it to the gun. Turn the power back on and force the thinner through by pulling the trigger. This will flush out any remaining paint. Shut down afterwards. You may need to repeat this until the gun is clear.

- Once the spray gun is free from coating/paint, remove the nozzle/air cap from the gun and clean it thoroughly again, using a lint-free cloth. Pay particular attention to the holes in the cap.

- Store everything in a dry, clean area ready for next use. Hang up the gun or lay it down in a drawer, preferably in its original packaging. Hang the paint lines up in a dry area on brackets or pegs.

Safety tip

Never point a spray gun at anyone while you are cleaning it or applying a coating. There are risks associated with the use of pressure.

Unit 2023

FAQ

Why do people spray paint rather than using brushes and rollers?

Spray painting gives a far superior finish, and is quicker and more cost-effective in the long run.

What sort of preparation do you need to do for spray painting?

Essentially, you need to do just the same as you would if you were brushing or rolling. You need to rub and brush down, wash down, fill etc. as is required. The only difference may be that you will need to mask very carefully, as the mist from spray painting can spread a long way.

Check it out

1 State and describe some of the considerations that need to be made when spray painting both internally and externally. Prepare a method statement explaining how best to prepare and work in both.

2 Explain how you should protect a polished floor before spraying.

3 Describe some of the factors that affect choice of spray system type, explaining why they are important for making a decision.

4 Explain how pressure is used in HVLP systems, stating the maximum pressure at which systems can operate.

5 Explain what the terms suction feed, gravity feed and pressure feed mean.

6 Sketch a diagram showing the component parts of a spray gun, explaining how each is used.

7 Prepare a method statement explaining how to set up and operate a spray gun and how to dismantle and store it after use.

8 Give two advantages and two disadvantages of using air-fed, filter and powered respirators and explain when you might decide to use each of these.

9 Explain why you should keep the correct distance between a surface and a spray gun when spraying.

10 Describe the process that should be used when spray painting around obstacles. What will you need to remember when following this process?

11 Describe three possible defects that can occur when spray painting and state steps you could put in place to prevent these from occurring.

12 Prepare a risk assessment for carrying out a spray painting task, explaining clearly the steps that need to be put in place to ensure that work is carried out safely.

Getting ready for assessment

The information contained in this unit, as well as the continued practical assignments that you will carry out in your college or training centre, will help you in preparing for both your end-of-unit test and the diploma multiple-choice test. It will also aid you in preparing for the work that is required for the synoptic practical assignments.

HVLP spray equipment is becoming increasingly common and is being used in a wide range of locations, not just industrial areas and jobs. You will need to be familiar with how these systems work, as well as the different safety and application implications that exist when using them. Your practical work will require you to be able to set up and use one of these machines to successfully complete a job.

You will need to be familiar with:

- preparing work areas by protecting surrounding areas, furniture and fittings
- setting up HVLP spray equipment and preparing materials for spray application
- applying water-based coatings by HVLP spray
- rectifying faults in spray equipment and defects in applied coatings
- cleaning, maintaining and storing HVLP spray equipment and materials. For learning outcome two you will need to be able to select the appropriate HVLP spray system type and identify and select the appropriate spray-gun component parts for particular jobs. You will need to be able to assemble these parts correctly, loading the paint material, testing and adjusting the equipment for use. In order to apply the paint correctly you will need to be able to check for correct air pressure at the nozzle, making sure that it meets environmental compliance. As always, you need to be sure that you are working to current health and safety regulations.

Before you carry out any work, you should outline your plan of action, which will tell you the order you need to do things in. It will also record a rough timescale for the work you need to carry out, in order to make sure that you complete everything you need to do safely. You will need to refer back to this plan at each stage to make sure that you are not making any mistakes as you work.

Your speed in carrying out any tasks in a practice setting will also help to prepare you for the time set for the test. However, you must never rush the test! Always make sure you are working safely. Make sure throughout the test that you are wearing the appropriate PPE and using tools correctly.

Good luck!

CHECK YOUR KNOWLEDGE

1 What are HAPs?

   a hard application powers

   b high altitude paints

   c hazardous air pollutants

   d hazardous air paints

2 If coatings become atomised, what happens to them?

   a the coating turns thick

   b the coating turns into a mist

   c the coating turns into jelly

   d none of the above

3 Why do painters prefer to use spray systems?

   a they save time

   b they are easy to clean

   c they are portable and lightweight

   d all of the above

4 How is paint applied when using an airless spray system?

   a compressed air

   b electricity

   c forcing paint through gun

   d mixing paint and air together

5 What are the main hazards a spray painter faces?

   a fumes, sprays and mists

   b manual handling injuries

   c falls

   d electrocution

6 How do you prevent blockages to a spray gun?

   a use a filter

   b use thinned out coatings

   c make sure correct maintenance is carried out

   d mix coatings correctly

7 If a mixing ratio is given as 75%, it means use

   a 1 part thinner, 4 parts paint

   b 2 parts thinner, 2 parts paint

   c 3 parts thinner, 4 parts paint

   d 4 parts thinner, 2 parts paint

8 What does viscosity mean with regard to coatings?

   a thickness

   b thinness

   c water based

   d solvent based

9 What is the recommended distance between the spray gun and the surface when applying coatings?

   a 50 cm to 1 m

   b as close as possible to the manufacturer's recommended distance

   c never less than 1 m

   d as close as possible

10 What happens when you arc the gun when spraying?

   a excessive overspray occurs

   b uneven finish

   c patchy finish

   d all of the above

Know how to erect and dismantle access equipment and working platforms 2

Most construction trades require frequent use of some type of working platform or access equipment, and painting and decorating is no different. Working off the ground can be very dangerous and the greater the height, the more serious the risk of injury. This unit will introduce you to some of the access equipment and working platforms you will use in order to work at height. It will also explain how to use these safely.

This unit contains material that supports NVQ unit QCF 250 Erect and dismantle access/working platforms.

This unit also contains material that supports TAP Unit Erect and dismantle access/working platforms.

This unit will cover the following learning outcomes:

- Interpreting guidance information for using access equipment and working platforms
- Calculating requirements to erect access equipment and working platforms
- Inspecting components, identifying defects and completing reports
- Erecting and working from access equipment and working platforms
- Dismantling and storing components

K1. Interpreting guidance information for using access equipment and working platforms

Suitable access equipment and working platforms

Stepladders and ladders

All types of ladders should only be set up on ground that is firm and level. All components should be checked fully before use, including checking to see if any repairs have been made. Don't use ladders to gain extra height on a working platform. There are some common safety checks for the materials that different types of ladder and stepladder can be made from.

Type of ladder	Safety issues
Wood	Check for loose screws, nuts, bolts and hinges. Check tie ropes are in good condition. Never paint as this will hide defects.
Aluminium	Avoid working near live electricity supplies.
Fibreglass	Once damaged, cannot be repaired and must be replaced.

Table 24.1 Ladders

Using a stepladder

Stepladders should only be used for work that will take a few minutes to complete. When work is likely to take longer, use a sturdier alternative. Always open the steps fully and check for the Kitemark (Figure 24.1), which shows that the ladder has been tested independently and audited to ensure it meets the appropriate standards.

Using ladders

The two most common types of ladder are pole ladder (single ladder) and extension ladder (ladders with two or more interlocking lengths).

Ladders are not designed for work of a long duration and should be secured in place. One hand should always be free to hold the ladder and you should not have to stretch while using it.

You should also observe the following points when erecting a ladder:

- Ensure at least a four-rung overlap on each extension section.
- Never rest on plastic guttering as it may break, causing the ladder to slip.

Figure 24.1 British Standards Institution Kitemark

- If the base of the ladder is exposed, guard it to prevent knocks.
- Secure the ladder at top and bottom. The bottom can be secured by a second person, but they must not leave while the ladder is in use.
- The angle of the ladder should be a ratio of 1:4 (or 75°) – see Figure 24.2.
- The top of the ladder must extend at least 1 m, or five rungs, above its landing point.

Trestle platforms

A trestle is a frame with a platform or other type of surface and should be used for work that will take longer than a few minutes to complete. It is made up of a frame and a platform. Always check platforms for damage. All trestles should only be used on level, firm ground. There are two main types of trestle:

- **A frame** – frame in the shape of a capital A, made from timber, aluminium or fiberglass. Two are used together to support a trestle platform. They should always be fully opened supporting a platform of not less than 450 mm. The overhang of the board should not be more than four times its thickness
- **Steel trestles** – sturdier than A-frames and adjustable in height, capable of supporting a wider platform. The trestles should not be more than 1.2 m apart.

Trestle platforms can have a number of boards depending on the size of the trestles.

Scaffolding

Tubular scaffold is the most commonly used type of scaffolding within the construction industry. There are two types of tubular scaffold:

- **independent scaffold** – free-standing and does not rely on the building to support it.
- **dependent scaffold** – attached to the building with poles (putlogs) inserted into the brickwork. The poles have a flattened end. They stay in position until work is complete and give the scaffold extra support.

Before using a scaffold you should assess its condition and suitability for the task.

Figure 24.2 Correct angle for a ladder

Figure 24.3 A-frame trestles with scaffold boards

Figure 24.4 Steel trestle with staging boards

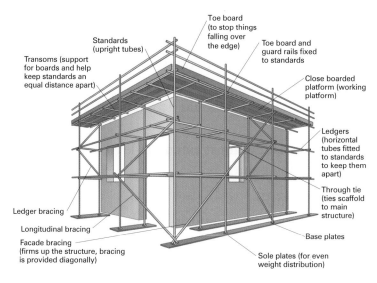

Figure 24.5 Components of a tubular scaffolding structure

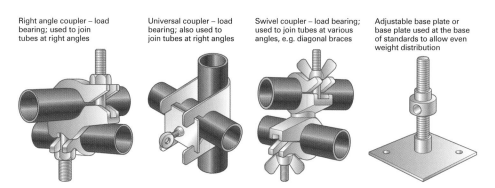

Figure 24.6 Types of scaffold fittings

Mobile tower scaffolds

Mobile tower scaffolds can be moved without being dismantled. They have lockable wheels and are used extensively by many different trades. They are made from either traditional steel tubes and fittings or aluminium, which is lightweight and easy to move. The aluminium type of tower is normally specially designed and is referred to as a 'proprietary tower'. A 'low tower' scaffold is designed for use by one person at 2.5 m height.

Tower scaffolds must have a firm and level base. The stability of the tower depends on the height in relation to the size of the base:

- for use inside a building, the height should be no more than three and a half times the smallest length
- for outside use, the height should be no more than three times the smallest base length.

All working platforms should be fitted with guard rails and toe boards on all four sides of the platform.

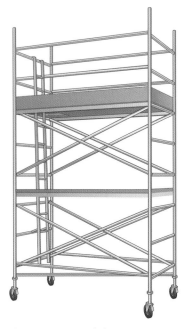

Figure 24.7 Mobile tower scaffold